I0787276

Wild Wood Magic:
A Guide to Walking as a Sacred Path

by Collin Stuart Chambers

Wild Wood Magic
A Guide to
Walking as a Sacred Path

by Collin Stuart Chambers

Copyright ©2021 Collin Stuart Chambers
All Rights Reserved. No part of this book may be reproduced
or used in any manner without the prior written permission
of the copyright owner, except for the use of brief
quotations in a book review.

Contact: collin@wildwoodmagic.com

Cover art: Collin Chambers
Design: John Pritchard

ISBN: 9798700639828
Library of Congress Control Number: 2021901790

WildwoodMagic.com

I dedicate this book to you.
May these words inspire you to be your healthiest,
happiest and most magical Self!

TABLE OF CONTENTS

Introduction..1

My Story: In the Beginning...3
   WHATEVER IT IS, SIGN ME UP!...4
   THE FREEDOM TRAIL..5
   WHERE IS THE MAGIC?..6
   FARAWAY MAGIC...8
   MADERA SALVAJE is WILD WOOD..9
   I SURRENDER..10
   FROM SURVIVAL TO THRIVING..11

Chapter 1

WHY WALK?...13
   WALKING IS AS NATURAL AS BREATHING..............................14
   WHY WALK?...14
   MENTAL, EMOTIONAL, & SPIRITUAL BENEFITS.....................15
   WALKING AS A SACRED PATH IS A MINDSET..........................16
   PHYSICAL HEALTH EQUALS INNER PEACE..............................16
   WALKING IS A PHYSICAL WAY TO ACCESS JOY.......................17
   RELEASE YOUR INNER CREATIVE ENERGY.............................18
   SHIFTING ENERGY THROUGH MOVEMENT...............................19

Chapter 2

WHAT IS WILDWOOD MAGIC?...21
   WHAT DOES "SACRED" MEAN? 22
   GOING WITH THE FLOW 22
   WALKING AS A SACRED PATH..23
   DEVELOPING AWARENESS 24
   WHAT IS WILDWOOD MAGIC?...25
   GUIDANCE IS EVERYWHERE...26
   NATURE IS WILDWOOD MAGIC!..27
   THE TALE OF RABBITS, SNAKES, HAWKS................................27
   WALKING CAN BE A MAGICAL ADVENTURE, EVEN IN THE CITY 28
   URBAN MAGIC: THE TALE OF THE SEVEN GOLD FOXES.......30
   LOW-TECH TIME 33
   HAVE YOU HEARD OF FOREST BATHING OR SHINRIN-YOKU? 33
   EVERYTHING IS A BLESSING! 34
   THE NOW IS HERE...35
   TRAIL MAGIC..36
   CAPTURING THE MAGIC WITH A CAMERA 36
   STREAM MAGIC: A MEDITATION 38

Chapter 3

CULTIVATING A SPIRITUAL DISCIPLINE:

TRY A 40-DAY SACRED PRACTICE.......................................39

THE SHIFT BEGINS THE MOMENT YOU COMMIT TO IT 40
DEVELOPING A MOVEMENT PRACTICE...40
CULTIVATING A SPIRITUAL DISCIPLINE 41
TRY A 40-DAY SACRED PRACTICE 42
DECIDE TO COMMIT 42
SELF-DISCIPLINE IS THE KEY TO FREEDOM......................................44
GUIDELINES FOR WALKING AS A SACRED PATH: 45
WALKING IS SELF-CARE..47

Chapter 4

OTHER SACRED PRACTICES 49

ANYTHING CAN BE A SACRED PRACTICE 50
MEDITATION 51
WHAT DOES MEDITATION DO?..52
YOGA 52
THE FOUNTAIN OF YOUTH: THE 5 TIBETAN RITES.................................53
DANCING: SACRED MOVEMENT 54
JOURNALING: WRITE IT DOWN!...55
PLAYING: IT'S NOT JUST FOR KIDS 56
LAUGHTER YOGA: IT'S A THING! 57
SMILES ARE GOLDEN: "GOOD STUFF SPREADS TOO!" 57
DIVINE EXPERIMENTATION..58

Chapter 5

BE A KEEPER OF THE LAND:
WALKING & HIKING ETIQUETTE 61

WALKING AND HIKING ETIQUETTE 63
WHAT IS "LEAVE NO TRACE," ANYWAY?...64
LEAVE NO TRACE SEVEN PRINCIPLES: 65
1. PLAN AHEAD AND PREPARE...65
2. TRAVEL AND CAMP ON DURABLE SURFACES....................................66
3. DISPOSE OF WASTE PROPERLY: "Pack it in, Pack it out!" 67
4. LEAVE WHAT YOU FIND..69
5. MINIMIZE CAMPFIRE IMPACTS..70
6. RESPECT WILDLIFE: 72

Chapter 6

THE HOW, WHERE & WITH WHOM OF IT ALL 77

THE NITTY GRITTY ON WALKING SAFETY: 78
WALKING GRACEFULLY 78
A FEW TIPS ON PROPER TECHNIQUE 79
SPEAK SOFTLY AND CARRY A BIG STICK... (OR HIKING POLES)....................80
AIM FOR 30 MINUTES PER DAY 81
WALKING WITH OTHERS 81
WALKING ALONE...82
IS IT SAFE TO WALK ALONE? 83
WALKING THE DOG...83
HOW TO FIND PEOPLE TO WALK WITH..84

FAMILIARITY ELIMINATES FEAR 85
LET YOUR BODY CHOOSE A PLACE TO WALK 85
NO, REALLY, WHERE SHOULD I WALK? 86
DIFFERENT TYPES OF TRAILS, PATHS, & TERRAIN 87
WALKING ON SIDEWALKS & OTHER FLAT SURFACES 88
LOOP TRAILS 88
OUT-AND-BACKS...89
LABYRINTHS: SACRED MOVING MEDITATION 89
EARTHING...THE HEALING MAGIC OF WALKING BAREFOOT...................89
LEARNING TO FLOW LIKE WATER: A MEDITATION 91

Chapter 7

WHAT SHOULD I BRING WITH ME? 93

THE SCOOP ABOUT HAULING STUFF ON A WALK 94
BEING PREPARED 94
THE OFFICIAL WILDWOOD MAGIC DAY-HIKING ESSENTIALS LIST: 95
DETAILED INFORMATION ABOUT THE GEAR IN THE LISTS 96
DAYPACKS 96
WAIST PACKS 97
FOOD 97
WHAT TO PACK TO EAT: CALORIES VS. NUTRITION...................................98
WATER 99
WATER CONTAINERS 100
COMPASS/MAP/HIKING GUIDE FOR THE AREA 101
CELL PHONE 101
HEADLAMP OR FLASHLIGHT 102
TOILET PAPER 103
FIRST AID AND GEAR REPAIR KIT 103
WATERPROOF MATCHES/LIGHTER AND FIRE STARTER 103
EXTRA CLOTHES 104
POCKETKNIFE OR MULTITOOL 104
HAND SANITIZER 104
BANDANA 105
EMERGENCY SHELTER 105
WHISTLE 105
WATER FILTER/PURIFIER OR CHEMICAL TREATMENT 105
ID/CASH/CREDIT CARD/HEALTH INSURANCE CARD/ITINERARY 106
WALKING STICK OR TREKKING POLES 106
SUNSCREEN/SUNGLASSES...106
TRASH BAG (OR A LARGE ZIPLOC BAG) FOR TRASH 107
WHAT SHOULD I WEAR? 107
ESSENTIAL CLOTHING: THINK IN LAYERS..107
HIKING SHOES OR BOOTS 107
GOOD QUALITY SOCKS 108
BASELAYER/BREATHABLE SHORT-SLEEVED SHIRT 108
QUICK-DRYING PANTS & SHORTS..109
SKIRTS & SKORTS 109
WATERPROOF/BREATHABLE RAIN JACKET AND PANTS.............................109
PONCHOS & OTHER RAIN ACCESSORIES..110

SUNHAT/WARM HAT AND GLOVES 110
INSULATED LAYER/JACKET...110
LONG UNDERWEAR/THERMALS/BASE LAYERS 110
CHOOSING THE RIGHT FABRIC   111
FABRICS... SYNTHETICS, SILK, AND WOOL.........................111
FABRICS... NYLON, POLYESTER, & STRETCHY STUFF 112

Chapter 8

I KNOW YOU ARE EXCITED ABOUT
A SECTION CALLED FEET!   113

APPRECIATE THE FEET!..114
SHOE-OFF BREAKS and OTHER EASY MIRACLE REMEDIES   115
FIND A GREAT MEDITATION SPOT 116
MANY PAINS IN THE BODY ORIGINATE FROM THE FEET! 117
OTHER QUICK FIXES: SHOE LACING OPTIONS 117
PUMICE-STONES, FOOT CREAM & FOOT POWDER 120
GET A PEDICURE!...121
DRY FEET ARE HAPPY FEET!...122
TIPS FOR WET SHOES & FEET:...123
HOW TO CHOOSE THE RIGHT PAIR OF SHOES OR BOOTS   124
FOOTWEAR: WHERE DO I START? 124
HOW TO BUY FOOTWEAR FOR WALKING & HIKING 125
NO PAIN, NO GAIN DOES NOT APPLY HERE! 125
TYPES OF WALKING, HIKING, & BACKPACKING FOOTWEAR 126
PARTS OF THE SHOE: THE MIDSOLE 127
PARTS OF THE SHOE: OUTSOLES 127
SOCKS & OTHER SHOE-RELATED ACCESSORIES   128
SOCKS 128
SOCK LINERS 129
SHOE INSERTS..129
HEEL CUPS 129

Chapter 9

WILD CREATURES AND BITEY THINGS   131

WALKING IN BEAR COUNTRY..132
WHAT DO I DO WHEN I SEE A BEAR?......................................133
OTHER STINGERS, RASHES, AND BITEY THINGS   134
BUGS and BITEY THINGS 134
AVOIDING THE BITEY THINGS...134
TREATING STINGS AND BITES 135
POISON IVY & OTHER ITCHY RASHES...................................136
AVOIDING THE ITCHY THINGS...137
HOW DO I TREAT A SNAKEBITE?...138
HOW DO I AVOID A SNAKEBITE?...138

Chapter 10

BASIC FIRST AID   141

FIRST AID KIT RECOMMENDATIONS 142

COMMON FIRST AID KIT CONTENTS 142
SUPERFICIAL WOUNDS, BLISTERS, AND BURNS....................................143
HOTSPOTS 144
FULL-ON BLISTERS...144
WOUNDS AND BURNS..146
SPRAINS, STRAINS, & BREAKS 148
HYPOTHERMIA..148
FROSTNIP/FROSTBITE 149
GEAR REPAIR KIT...149

Conclusion

ARE YOU READY FOR THE REAL MAGIC? 151

Acknowledgements 153

About the Author 157

Introduction

Once upon a time....
Isn't that how you are supposed to begin a grand story? Well, ok.
Here goes...

Once upon a time, you couldn't even get me to go for a walk. A
short while later, I walked regularly, but I still thought it was
just a calorie-burning chore called "exercise." Now, I can look
back and honestly say, walking unquestionably saved my life in
more ways than I can count. Not only for all the weight loss
and health benefits, but also the more subtle and less quantifi-
able value it creates. It is within these elusive and inexplicable
rewards that we find exactly what we need, intricately woven
throughout the challenging path of self-transformation.

In the pages that follow, I first take you through my own journey
and how I came to realize the significance of this miraculous gift.
I keep hearing myself tell people that this book has been "a lifetime in the making," and, indeed, it is. But in actuality, I needed
every one of the ups, downs, failures, victories, trauma, and
drama to show me how walking *always* heals and calms my soul.
It is my wish that this story will show you that no matter what
your life is like now, walking can greatly enhance it for the better.

I describe the physical, mental, and spiritual benefits as best as
possible within the limitations of the written word. I hope to
inspire you to add this most basic movement to your own life,
and I show you how to do it effortlessly. I thoroughly cover all
the relevant how's, why's, where's, what's, and with who's, as
well as how to make walking a *Sacred Ritual* that builds self-
confidence and wellbeing.

However, words fall miserably short. Walking is a most uncom-
plicated activity, but this approach to walking is also an experi-

ential one. Until you experiment for yourself, possibly even commit to a *40-day Practice* as suggested, you will never know the true worth.

What is unique about this book on such an ordinary subject such as taking a walk, is the invitation to perceive such tasks with renewed eyes. There is an energy about everything we do, which can be summed up in the word "intention." If you explore the natural world... the *WildWood,* as I like to call it... in a whimsical and playful manner, an extraordinary transformation trickles into every facet of daily life.

I have written this book as if you asked me what I thought was the ultimate ingredient for a happy, healthy, and radiant life. Prepare to fall in love with *Walking as a Sacred Path,* as this could be what you have been searching for all along. Please know that when you consider any of the thoughts discussed in this book, my loving support is always with you.

Love, Collin

My Story: In the Beginning

My daily walks,
which I consider my most treasured spiritual practice,
help me feel fully alive,
inspire my creativity,
awaken my Spirit,
and reveal the wondrous magic all around us,
everywhere!

I have always been a curious seeker of adventure... the more magical and mysterious, the better. As a young girl, you could always find me playing outside, deep in some kind of imaginary and thrilling venture. My past is now something I truly appreciate because of the wisdom, experiences, and skills that I acquired -often learned the hard way- and I embrace playfulness with all my heart.

I am sure my mother would tell you my wild escapades began the day I was born. Rebellious and defiant, I chose my path from the very beginning. Not one for following directions or appreciating the value of structured education, I began sliding down a slippery slope at an early age. I had emotional problems as well as body image issues, even as an adolescent. In high school, it became evident I had severe drug and alcohol troubles, as well as a blossoming weight problem.

WHATEVER IT IS, SIGN ME UP!

By college, I had tried just about every diet fad, pill, miracle gadget, exercise program, Jenny Craig, Weight Watchers, Nutri-System, cabbage soup diet, and "Guaranteed to lose weight or your money back" gimmick there was. I was the quintessential mascot of the yo-yo dieter. During my tumultuous youth, I lost 50 pounds three times, gaining back even more, each time, before finally hitting rock bottom. My life sucked, and I was totally miserable.

At age 26, still disgusted and depressed, and all on my own, I conquered my worst addictions and lost over 100 pounds. In the beginning, all I knew is that I was obese, I hated the gym, and I loved being outside. My parents had always been avid walkers and runners, so it was an obvious choice when I got bored with my "Dancing to the Oldies" VHS tape. (Thank you, Richard Simmons!) Because I had been nothing short of utterly obsessed with losing weight for years, beating myself up the entire time, I finally realized it was, in fact, all about my lack of acceptance and self-love. Then began the arduous journey of learning self-care.

When I first began the practice of walking, sacred it was not. Or, so I thought. Starting an exercise program when you are technically "morbidly obese" is intimidating all by itself. It wasn't until I gave up fast food, hard drugs, alcohol, and ciga-rettes... oh, and hating myself... that the weight came off and stayed off. That was when I started walking- every day. Walk-ing was the last thing I ever "tried" to lose weight.
Walking was the not-so-secret ingredient I had been looking for, and it was right under my nose the whole time. I quickly found it was so much more than just a physical activity or the dreaded word "exercise." I began to have confidence I had nev-er known and a sense of accomplishment I didn't know was even possible. Shortly after starting my daily walks, motivation easily came as I saw the pounds begin to drop.

THE FREEDOM TRAIL
I lived in various places all over the Southeast, but it wasn't un-til the mid-90s when I moved back to my hometown of Atlanta, Georgia, in the super funky neighborhood of Little Five Points, that I discovered a really cool place to walk. I found it is possi-ble to find magic and wonder in the city, too. The Freedom Trail was a pedestrian path that allowed me to walk many miles safely around the city, mostly surrounded by nature. It was the perfect place to take a long walk.

Living in Atlanta again was when I had some of the most disci-plined walking and running routines of my life. It was training in my Atlanta neighborhood that inspired me to run the famous Peachtree Road Race and, later, a half-marathon. Those were notable accomplishments for me because it was the first time in my life that I had ever actually felt the least bit athletic.

It is also where I was so motivated to get *out* of the city that I began driving up to the mountains to hike. Every. Single. Weekend. All I wanted to do was explore hiking trails that I would read about all week while daydreaming at work. So yes, that's right, I moved from Asheville, N.C., surrounded by beautiful mountains, but never hiked, back to Atlanta, G.A., where I literally drove back up to the mountains every weekend to hike. I love irony.

I finally recognized that this passion for getting outside and leading others into the wilderness truly motivated me. So, I decided to walk away from everything- a steady income with a great career, good benefits, and security, a loving family and friends, a large house with a pool, to live in a tiny one-bedroom cabin, and open and operate a hiking shop in the north Georgia mountains. Of course, opening a retail business around your most passionate pursuit can have real consequences. The ones like, oh...I don't know...you never get to do your favorite thing again because you're too busy running a business? Or something like that.

> *"And into the forest I go to lose my mind and find my soul."*
> —John Muir

WHERE IS THE MAGIC?

Life felt so tedious and boring, even though I owned my dream business. I kept thinking to myself, "Where is the magic?" The nine-to-six workaday world felt like a cruel life sentence that was suffocating my lighthearted Spirit. I was so ready to put all my wildest dreams and ideas into action. And that I did. In 2009, I left the husband, sold my backpacking and hiking business, and put all my belongings in storage to thru-hike the 2,200-mile Appalachian Trail.

My life changed forever on that cold March day at the top of Springer Mountain. I began a journey that would test me to my core- six months of the most difficult journey I had ever known, as well as the most rewarding and liberating! The daily sense of accomplishment getting myself 15, 20, or 25 miles further along this demanding path kept me going despite physical pain and mental stress.

Oh, did I learn a lot! Most importantly, I realized that I could count on myself, no matter what. When I found myself in daunting situations, instead of having emotional breakdowns, I found the ability to stay grounded and muster courage out of thin air, which came easier each time I faced a new challenge. I never realized how powerful I was! I now know I can do anything!

What started as an arduous physical test of endurance turned into a gratifying system of whole health- mentally, spiritually, and physically, only by walking in nature and being present. The simple beauty of walking, with only the purpose of walking, every day, opened my eyes in a way I never suspected and filled me with wonder and gratitude. When I arrived six months later, at the northern terminus of the Appalachian Trail, Mount Katahdin, my journey was only just beginning.

After I sold the hiking and backpacking shop, hiked a really long trail, divorced the second husband, and put all my belongings in storage, ...again..., I was ready to find out what life had to offer next. I was humorously calling this new phase of life an *Experiment in Trust,* as I booked a one-way ticket to Peru. I called myself an *Experimentalist* because I have frequently embraced radical and total transformation. Kind of like throwing all your cards in the air and starting life entirely over. Decades of trying new things, visiting and moving to new places, meeting new people, new jobs, new businesses, new hobbies, quitting addictions, losing weight, and starting a new life was nothing new to this wild and free Spirit.

FARAWAY MAGIC

My curiosity and desire to bring more magic and mystery into my life propelled me to take further leaps of faith. The intuitive messages and signs I received more and more frequently showed me an exhilarating path was calling me. I was divinely led to mystical Peru, where for nearly a year, I immersed myself in yoga, energy medicine, shamanic healing rituals, and ancient Incan magic. Peru awakened my own style of magic in every way possible. I felt something greater calling to me and began a journey that was nothing short of an enchanted fairytale, teaching me to remain open and trust where life enticed me to go.

The first few weeks in Peru were a whirlwind of phenomenal experiences as part of a spiritual retreat, but after that, I had no idea what I was supposed to be doing there. Absolutely none... just a backpack, a whole bunch of enthusiastic curiosity, and the desire to find the proverbial enchanted forest. My experiment serendipitously landed me in a village in the Sacred Valley of Cusco, living in a community of extraordinary people, having amazing experiences daily that would forever change my life.

My domesticated life was all but a distant memory, as I signed up for my first yoga teacher training, Reiki classes, apprenticeships, and workshops, the likes of which I had never imagined. Oh yeah, and a limitless supply of cheap bus tickets to incredible adventures throughout South America. It was as if I had just traded in endless humdrumness for the most charmed life I could ever imagine. I was living a true-to-life fairytale, complete with a palace, magic wands, fairies, and good witches.

AWAKENER OF MAGIC

I had nothing to compare life to in such otherworldly realms, as I suddenly found myself participating in all sorts of healing ceremonies initiating many magical synchronicities. I was given an open invitation to free my long-repressed wild Spirit to come out and play with the wide-eyed wonder of a child on Christmas.

I would walk by the river and find pieces of wood that beck-
oned me to turn them into magic wands in the little art studio I
created in my space. Eventually, I began to host sacred ceremonies of my own. In one such event, in an ancient Incan tem-
ple, I received the title, *Awakener of Magic*, from a dear friend.
I gratefully received this and accepted it as a divine calling.
And I have never looked back.

MADERA SALVAJE is WILD WOOD
In another ceremony, I made my way back to our circle with an
armful of sticks that a beautiful friend called out, "Madera!"
which means *wood* in Spanish. I am not exactly sure how it
happened, but everyone just called me Madera from that day
forward. It was at the top of the sacred Apu, (mountain spirit)
Machu Picchu herself, that I was gifted the second part of my
spirit name, "Salvaje," which means *wild*. I was so honored and
thrilled to have received this sacred name that I decided to
change my name to Madera Salvaje, *Wild Wood*.

After Peru, I was eager to continue following the breadcrumbs
of Spirit. I went to Thailand, where I lived in a modern-day
mystery school, learning ancient women's practices and cere-
monial rituals. It was here that I discovered the power of our
inherent divine feminine nature. I recognized my inner
strength and beauty through the art of *Mystical Dance* with a
tribe of absolutely amazing women. It was there that I uncov-
ered the beauty of *Sacred Movement*, the dance we all have
within, that moves through us, not so much as performance,
but an expression of our divine being. Through this elemental
dance, as well as my daily walks, I was finally learning to love
my body.

My inspirational path led me to India, where I lived in an
ashram rigorously learning traditional Tantra yoga for six
months. The ceremonies, rituals, and yoga I learned in that little village south of Goa are some of my beloved spiritual prac-

tices to this day. I clearly saw how the discipline of my daily rituals positively influenced the outcome of my day. The gift of this experience was learning the importance of self-love through mastery and self-discipline.

After bidding farewell to India, I found myself in Nepal, where I practiced new and different meditations and yoga styles. Trekking in the Himalayas was nothing like I had ever experienced. I serendipitously found a delightful guide who helped me experience the wild and rugged side of this fantastic place- exploring these giant mountains and charming little villages, day after day. Nepal felt ancient and primordial and reminded me once again how walking in nature can be an extraordinary and life-changing way to practice being present.

I SURRENDER
When I ultimately made it back to the United States, to the south more specifically, I could not understand why Americans could not correctly pronounce the beautiful word *Madera*. It would come out something like, "Muhdeeeeeera." To me, it was awful, like the sound of fingernails on a chalkboard. I also found it quite amusing, but dreadful, nonetheless. And so, I accepted the fact that Madera Salvaje had somehow lost her Peruvian magic traveling back through the portal to America. But it wasn't *Madera* who had lost her magic! Life was so different, no longer being surrounded by the people and places that helped me cultivate such a passionately different lifestyle. Most people only saw me as the person I was before I left, all those years earlier. They had no clue I had fallen down the proverbial rabbit hole into an enchanted land, lived a veritable lifetime as a wholly different person, and then showed up again, out of the blue, with a strange name that no one could pronounce.

It was a frustrating and confusing time, to say the least. I suddenly felt lost and unrooted. Life had seemed so exciting and purposeful while living in so many different cultures in my real-life fairytale. However, it wasn't long before I realized that I truly wanted to inspire people to see their own inner magic, right here, in America. And so, began my work.

I facilitated workshops and ceremonies attempting to recreate the magic that seemed to be ubiquitous and effortless in the places from which I had just returned. Although it wasn't even close to being the same, it still felt like very important work. I didn't have a clue back then where it would take me!

After contemplating my mystical explorations and ending up essentially where I had started, I began to realize the truth. I instantly return to this magical state of being when I am *walking in the woods*. Forests have always been my genuine happy place, no matter the country or continent. Many of us feel powerfully guided and supported by the nurturing company of Mother Nature herself.

This awareness was the most magnificent epiphany. It wasn't only the ancient ruins, temples, and hidden villages that held the magic; the magic lives within us all! When I walk in the woods, I am instantly transported to an enchanted land. And no matter what name I am called, I can summon this mystical place and profound experiences any time I wish. It is merely my perspective. And it is as real as the shoes on my feet.

FROM SURVIVAL TO THRIVING

Experiencing the magic and mystery of these mystical cultures proved that it is wholly within my power to create a truly extraordinary life. I have learned to listen to and trust my intuition and the wisdom of my body. I now gratefully nourish my whole Self in every way that supports thriving, not just surviving.

And that leads me back to simply taking a walk. Walking can take us on a thrilling journey, any time, any place. In this, the everyday-ordinary world, it is the simple things that can be the most significant and transformational. The magic is our ability to see beyond the illusion of the mundane. It does not take any special skills, knowledge, or plane tickets to faraway places. You already have everything you need.

Walking as a Sacred Path can help heal, balance, and transform anything we experience daily, whether physical, mental, or spiritual. This book is the result of a wild and cosmic dance spanning many decades, countless lessons, and amazing adventures in enchanted lands near and far.

I believe I am here on this earth to share the journey of walking and how profoundly it can change your life. I hope to inspire you on a fun and whimsical path of personal transformation, health, and happiness. The *Magic of the Wild Wood* is everywhere you seek it. So, find your enchanted forest and take a walk. Your life will be forever changed, for the better!

Chapter 1
WHY WALK?

What is magic?
It is everywhere you look.
The answer must be simple,
And walking is it.
Pursuits are waiting for you
to find your unique way,
And they are most fitting just for you.
When you investigate with an unguarded mind,
the places appear.
Or rather, you are mysteriously drawn to them.
And then you begin to see mention again somewhere,
in some other way.
And this is the Universe opening a door for you,
a Sacred exploration for you, alone.
Like a mystical quest... straight out of a fairytale.
We ponder with ears and eyes wide open.
Alongside Awe and much Gratitude
we infinitely consider these things.

WALKING IS AS NATURAL AS BREATHING

It has been a long journey getting to the place where I am no longer searching for the movement that my body intuitively enjoys and wants to do. Walking is such a natural thing. It is the movement we were all designed to do. Literally, we are made for walking. There is no surprise that it feels good and natural to walk at a comfortable pace, especially in a beautiful place. It requires no special clothing, no equipment, except for some good shoes and socks, takes minimal effort, and you can do it for free at any time, almost anywhere.

Walking is also a splendid activity because most people can do it. One of the most significant accomplishments of a toddler, we later forget how such a simple act can be so transformational. Even adding just a short walk to your everyday routine can be life-changing.

Walking, for most people, is as natural as breathing. Somehow in our modern-day quest for convenience and comfort, we have evolved to mostly sitting. Today's sedentary lifestyle is a growing concern. The adverse effects on human health are numerous, and wholly preventable diseases are now commonplace because of the amount of time we spend sitting. How did we get here?

> *"Now shall I walk, or shall I ride?*
> *'Ride,' Pleasure said;*
> *'Walk,' Joy replied."*
> —W.H. Davies

WHY WALK?

I walk every day I possibly can. It isn't just a habit that compels me to don my hiking shoes and hit the trail, street, beach, or wherever there is to walk nearby. It is my inherent desire to be outside, move my body, and find whatever nature magic is out there waiting for me to show up. There are so many compelling reasons to go for a walk. Beyond leaving your stresses behind for a while, going for a walk generates profound peace, whole health, and personal freedom.

Walking is the answer for many people to ensure overall good health, physically, mentally, emotionally, and spiritually. Some of the physical benefits are weight loss, higher energy levels, stronger muscles and bones, decreased blood pressure, and less chance of heart problems, osteoporosis, arthritis, cancer, obesity, and diabetes, just to name a few. Scientists and researchers now have linked walking with a reduction in many conditions, everything from cognitive decline to sexual dysfunction. It is a nearly perfect panacea!

Walking also improves coordination and balance, eases joint pain, boosts the immune system, and can even motivate you to choose healthier eating options, such as decreased sugar cravings. There is so much scientific research now that confirms the endless benefits of one of the simplest activities on Earth, walking!

> *"Look deep into nature, and then you will*
> *understand everything better."*
> —Albert Einstein

MENTAL, EMOTIONAL, & SPIRITUAL BENEFITS
There is an equally long list of mental, emotional, and spiritual benefits as well, such as elevated mood, reduced stress, a sense of accomplishment, and a deeper connection to nature. Movement naturally energizes our whole Self, not just our physical organs, blood, bones, and tissue. Our chakras, or energy centers, are stimulated by the harmonious movement, and our spirit is restored and renewed.

Walking is an effective moving meditation and can be easier and more comfortable for many than a sitting meditation. I have come to regard this activity as my most profound spiritual discipline. It elevates my connection to Spirit and reveals the divine beauty all around, everywhere. Gentle movement keeps our minds and hearts open, ready to experience the ever-present gifts life has to offer.

The self-confidence that comes with adding a daily walking practice is considerable, no matter how little time you spend doing it. Merely holding yourself accountable for adding self-care to your routine will benefit you in countless ways. In time, we naturally begin to make other small self-improvement changes, like choosing more nutritious food, saying no to sugar, drinking more water, and maybe even more restful sleep. It is a genuine self-care domino effect.

WALKING AS A SACRED PATH IS A MINDSET
Walking as a Sacred Path is the mental attitude and emotional mindset you carry with you when you walk out the door. It changes the entire walking experience. When I first began walking, it was only for exercise. I was obsessed with burning calories, which is why I started running, well, jogging was more like it, but whatever.

I realize now, with crystal clear hindsight, that my intense calorie-burning mentality, complete with injuries and much suffering, made my journey so much more difficult than ever was necessary. I had not dealt with any of the emotional issues that caused me to put the weight on in the first place.

PHYSICAL HEALTH EQUALS INNER PEACE
Our bodies are the physical representations of our inner state of being, like a mirror. When there is dis-ease, injury, pain, or discomfort within the body, there is an emotional imbalance that is ultimately responsible. There is a direct and undeniable

correlation between the path of inner peace and the relation-ship between physical movement and nourishment.

Whether you are trying to lose weight, gain confidence, get clarity, feel self-reliant, or be more peaceful, they all require a mindset shift. Leaving out the most essential ingredients of self-love and acceptance is a guaranteed failure. Embrace the attitude that you are in the perfect place, at the perfect time, and you are already well on your way to health and happiness. Taking a walk every day for the sheer delight of it satisfies all the requirements for a healthy mind, body, and spirit.

> *"All truly great thoughts are conceived while walking. "*
> —Friedrich Nietzsche

WALKING IS A PHYSICAL WAY TO ACCESS JOY
It is the absolute truth. Walking is indeed an ideal way to ac-cess joy! I'm not talking about some fly-by-night cheap thrill here. I'm talking about the pure indwelling joy inherent in every being who gets flung into this world... overflowing with giddy glee. Even if you are saying right now, in your head, "I don't have that," the Universe says otherwise. It just looks completely different in every person. Guess what? That means you get to make up your own crazy-unique version! [Cue ma-niacal laughter]

Bliss is our inherent birthright. We quickly forget this as we leave behind our childhood innocence and begin learning "the right way" to act, what is proper to believe, and whatnot. Or, so our subconscious minds think. Walking, a lot like tapping, yoga, tai chi, drumming, or any physical movement-based medi-tation or activity, instantaneously stimulates many positive processes within the body.

The word "yoga" means "to unite," such as in mind, body, and spirit. Walking is precisely the same medicine. The physical activity of walking frees the mind and lifts the spirit. A simple repetitive movement loosens blocked, stagnant emotion and clears the way for new, shiny perspectives to enter. This is quickly self-evident when taking a walk when you have heavy, negative feelings. Soon you realize that you feel much better, and it doesn't even take that much time. I double-dog-dare you to try it.

> ***"If you are in a bad mood, go for a walk.***
> ***If you are still in a bad mood, go for another walk."***
> —Hippocrates

RELEASE YOUR INNER CREATIVE ENERGY

Walking is a fantastic way to release the creative energy that is not being channeled elsewhere in our lives. Our creativity, just like the powerful sexual energy within every human body, is our outward expression of the Self. Creativity is not just relegated to "art" or "reproduction." Creative energy could be anything, such as the way we prepare a delectable dish, tend to a garden, teach our little ones, or any place we use our intuitive, imaginative forces.

If we do not release this mighty and powerful force, it can turn inward and behave as a destructive power. This blockage often shows up as addiction, anger, depression, and so forth. Thankfully, walking can be an immediate and effective remedy for negative emotions and suppressed creative energy.

> ***After a day's walk, everything has twice its usual value."***
> —George Macauley Trevelyan

SHIFTING ENERGY THROUGH MOVEMENT
Many of our issues can be lessened by returning to those creative endeavors that speak to us the most. Our music, art, writing, or maybe something entirely new that you haven't even tried yet, is calling out to you. The world is your oyster. You are never too old, too fat, too skinny, too poor, or too anything to make it happen. All you have to do is want it, believe it is possible, and take *inspired action*. As cliché as that may sound, it is the truth. And it all begins with movement.

To move past life's sometimes daily stumbling blocks, often we simply need to shift our energy. The easiest way to shift our energetic body is to *move* our physical body. Fortunately, it does not take too much to make this happen. We can do just about anything that moves the body, whether it is sweeping the front porch, turning on some music, and getting your boogie-woogie on right there in the kitchen.... or just go right outside your front door and take a walk.

Sometimes we don't feel very "creative." For whatever reason, if we do not think we have, what many would label as artistic gifts, physical movement can alter this flow of energy, too. The bottom line is, humans are meant to move. Moving our bodies allows our life force energy to flow freely through us. This sets off a chain reaction of physiological effects, that in turn, create mental and spiritual inspiration that can profoundly change our life.

Or not.

On the other hand, not moving our bodies promotes stress and a multitude of problems that accumulate over time. A sedentary life solidifies tension and stagnates our energy, among other adverse effects. By holding on to stress, we allow it to settle deep within our body, making us feel sick, tired, and weak. Although any movement will do, I believe walking is the easiest, most accessible, and has abundant benefits. I wrote this line in a journal many years ago, *"There is nothing I can't make better by taking a walk."* And I still believe it to this day.

Chapter 2
WHAT IS WILDWOOD MAGIC?

Why walk?
Well, that's easy.
To Be Here Now, of course.
Can you hear the babbling brook?
Can you hear the Pileated Woodpecker calling your name?
Are you inspired to frolic to the song of your own drumbeat?
The beauty of walking is the simplicity itself.
In the busy bee world around us, we are tempted into confusion,
overwhelmed by infinite homemade complexity.
We are lured by shiny new things to coax us out of
our humdrumness.
But it really is nearly effortless.
...And cures all that ails,
with the very first step outside the door.

WHAT DOES "SACRED" MEAN?

It is not essential to believe in any religion, particular path, deity, or God to have a connection with the *Sacred*. Sacred refers to the universal life force found in and connects all things, seen and unseen. When we intentionally tap into the element of Divine Love (Source, Higher Self, Universe... whatever name you prefer), we are choosing to see life through the whimsical lens of the extraordinary. From a place of deep reverence, we embark on an inward journey, with renewed eyes and open hearts, to find a deeper connection in our exploration of Self and the beliefs that define us. The more we come from this sacred space within, the more real magic is revealed to us.

GOING WITH THE FLOW

There is a recognizable energy about the way we do everything. We can drive fast and aggressively, or we can drive calmly and feel relaxed. We can eat hastily while we are distracted, or we can chew mindfully and make eating a healing ritual. The same goes for any activity, including walking.

We do things the way we do them because that is how we were taught to do them. Or... how we consciously *choose* to do them. The choice is always ours to make. When we are in the flow, responding instead of reacting, we are in a state of surrender, like watching a movie going on all around us. We choose how we go about everything, and it all comes back to our intention.

When we choose to walk in a calm and relaxed way, allowing the terrain to guide us gently, the experience is such that each footstep feels effortless and purposefully positioned. We do not have to awkwardly battle a twisty trail or stumble over obstacles that seem to appear before us suddenly. It is the energy and intention of the effort put forth that creates our state of being. With a receptive attitude, we may flow down the path with an open heart, as if we are one with it.

When we are *Walking as a Sacred Path*, we are aligned with Spirit and one with the Earth. Our movement becomes light and less restricted. If we can lessen our tight grip on the stresses of the day, the experience itself surrounds us and leads us on a sacred journey. Walking as a meditation fills all the voids and answers all the questions from a place of freedom.

With gratitude for all her gifts, walking in awe of nature's beauty is a habit we can learn to cultivate. In the beginning, it might take getting yourself physically in a place that you find delightful to fully immerse yourself in a new practice. And then, one day, out of the blue, you will have the most miraculous experiences! And just like that, as if by magic, life outside of walking yields similar qualities, and inner peace prevails in all hours of the day.

WALKING AS A SACRED PATH
Whether you are an experienced hiker or walking a path for the first time, I invite you to consider walking like a sacred ceremony of *Awakening*. By approaching the simple act of taking a walk from a place of gratitude and holy connection to our natural world, we are opening ourselves to a powerful energy that flows through all life. This Divine Source Energy is perpetually shifting and evolving, just as we are.

Whether it is an urban neighborhood, beach, or shaded woodland trail, the land it meanders through has called us there. Nearby is something just for us, patiently waiting for us to notice. In this ritual of *Walking as a Sacred Path*, we are inspired, healed, and supported by the Earth and all her magic. We are guided in a way perfectly fitting for all our needs and desires.

Like learning the meditation practice of observing the breath, *Walking as a Sacred Path* stimulates seeing, listening, and *being* from a place well beyond the eyes and ears. Being present in nature, open to receive all of the inspiration, answers, and guidance we seek, is a practice worth cultivating.

DEVELOPING AWARENESS

The first step in cultivating a *Sacred Walking Practice* is to set the intention to develop active *Awareness*. Begin by being mindful as you move through your day. It is the art of just *being,* right where we are, alert and observing, without any sort of judgment. Awareness is repeatedly embracing the present moment while consciously releasing distractions, one moment at a time.

Our intention creates our reality. So, if our intention is to become more aware, we will begin to notice things we may not have otherwise seen because, well, we asked to see them! When we ask the universe for guidance, we always receive it. Because we are being given guidance through a variety of signs and symbols all the time, with vigilant attentiveness, we can naturally allow these experiences to present themselves to us.

When we become aware of a sign, it is the *significance* that we place on the message that becomes our guidance. It is our choice to trust this communication or discard it as mere coincidence or odd happenstance. If it feels like you are making it all up, feel at ease in knowing the divine works creatively though our imagination. It is always our choice to receive and interpret the gifts and blessings we are continuously being offered. Awakening to this truth allows our awareness to lead us to the magic that is, indeed, all around us.

Awareness is also becoming more in tune with our physical bodies. Sometimes, we numb ourselves to thoughts and beliefs that feel uncomfortable and know very little about what is actually going on in our own bodies. Having body wisdom begins to reveal accumulated emotions and stress we may not even realize we are holding. We often internalize painful emotions that do not get actively released and later show up as dis-ease. Many of us anesthetize these uncomfortable feelings with food, drink, sugar, sex, tv, devices, and a myriad of other addictions. Intentionally becoming more mindful will allow hidden thoughts and beliefs to surface, initiating the path to healing.

DOING AND BEING

We are so busy trying to figure out what we are supposed to be "doing" that we fail to notice that our "doing" often gets in the way of our being. We don't have to figure anything out. When I walk in the woods, the next right thing to *do* just comes to me without thought. It is as if my very movement pulls creative ideas right up from the ground below and flows directly into my mind from the sky above. The movement awakens my creativity and joins together the fragments of my soul that have been folded awkwardly under a desk for far too many hours.

"I am alarmed when it happens that I have walked a mile into the woods bodily, without getting there in spirit."
—Henry David Thoreau

WHAT IS WILDWOOD MAGIC?

The *Wild Wood* is an enchanted place where we take our physical body for a simple walk in the woods and are, in turn, gifted with nothing less than a profound experience. We enter the *Magic of the WildWood,* in essence, through our purpose or intention.

We allow the elements of the natural world to permeate our being and transport us to another realm of existence. We are continuously invited to go beyond our senses to embrace what we cannot see or hear with the eyes or ears. There is a miraculous world out there, speaking to us in every moment through flora and fauna, signs and symbols, and synchronistic moments, anticipating our *Awakening.* If you look for the magic, you will most certainly find it.

Within the intricate wonder of a spider's web, the sudden whirr of a tiny hummingbird, or an amusing character looking back at you from a knot in a tree ...magic is everywhere. It is a perspective we *choose* to welcome, as if we were peeking through the keyhole of an alternate reality. We can view life as an endless series of tedious tasks or a captivating and whimsical playground, where we can create anything we desire, purely by focusing upon it. By choosing to view the world through this magical lens, the veil begins to lift.

GUIDANCE IS EVERYWHERE

Nature spirits, guides, angels, and other benevolent, loving beings can be our personal guides and council. Teachers of all kinds surround us, and they are thrilled to walk beside us, providing gentle support whenever we ask. You may begin to have epiphanies, downloads, illuminations, or *Aha!* moments more frequently. They appear to come from nowhere, when in fact, these inspired revelations are coming *through us,* from the Divine, Source, Creator, or Great Spirit. We can encourage more synchronicities and messages by bringing ourselves back to the present moment and tuning in to that indwelling guidance within. Walking is a most enjoyable way to access this profound and ancient wisdom.

When we ask, it is always given. Divine assistance is readily available and is only an inquiry away. The answers do not always show up exactly as we would have them, but a reply is sure to come. When we remain open to the mystery and allow our intuition to govern our state of being, instead of subconscious, fear-based thoughts, we find peace and freedom. Freedom comes when we let go of control and surrender to life.

Mother Nature whispers in our ears as we take another step with anticipation and quickening senses. Wild winged ones sing their songs to us, sparkling colors invite us in, and shapes and patterns disclose their ancient mysteries for all to see. We are surrounded by teachers, elders, healers, and benevolent guides in the *Wild Wood*. And when we begin to pay attention, they reveal their secrets in earnest.

NATURE IS *WILDWOOD MAGIC!*

One of my favorite authors, Ted Andrews, defines himself as a "Spiritist," which he describes as somebody that believes the world is filled with divine and expressive spirits that can relate to and communicate with humans. I think this concept is in perfect alignment with *WildWood Magic*.

Spending time in nature has taught me that all I have to do is open my eyes to see delightful miracles all around. me. I understand my relationship with nature to be a choice I have made. The result is that I have enchanted encounters continuously with the wonders of the natural world. I also understand this to be a gift anyone can choose to nurture. We can learn to see the magic and mystery all around us. It is simply having an open mind and choosing to see it and believe it.

THE TALE OF RABBITS, SNAKES, HAWKS
& OTHER MAGICAL CREATURES

I have a special friend that when we get together, we always have remarkable and otherworldly experiences. And although we expect to have extraordinary adventures together, it never ceases to delight and amaze me. One trip was particularly amazing. One morning on our walk, we happened upon a snake on the side of the trail in the grass. Although many people are frightened of snakes and have fearful reactions, I view snakes as powerful symbols of healing, transformation, and rebirth. I always cherish my encounters with snakes.

It was the most peaceful and beautiful encounter with a timber rattlesnake we could have ever imagined. As she slithered slowly and methodically, in a straight line toward the other side of the gravel roadbed, we were able to watch her safely from a distance with awe and gratitude. My entire being was filled with excitement to be witness to this experience. We both knew it was a special sign.

During the trip's progression, filled with many awe-inspiring events, I knew that treating this snake encounter as the magical healing event that it was, had allowed us to receive many more blessings. After that, we had other experiences with fawns, hawks, and rabbits that seemed just as astonishing. Each time we would take time to stop and ask what the message was. And the answers always came, loud and clear. We all can receive guidance whenever we need it, and it can be most exhilarating!
With *awareness*, we are given opportunities to awaken a whole new world within ourselves. Sometimes it takes an authentic *leap of faith* to believe in serendipitous circumstances instead of labeling them accidental or mere coincidences. If we can open our minds and senses to this enchanted world hiding in plain sight, we are rewarded with awe and beauty. What magic have you seen today?

> **"Everywhere we look,**
> **complex magic of nature blazes before our eyes."**
> —Vincent Van Gogh

WALKING CAN BE A MAGICAL ADVENTURE, EVEN IN THE CITY
There is plenty of magic to be found in urban walking adventures, too. There are social benefits, as well. Walking through your neighborhood allows you to have a much deeper understanding of who lives around you. I love walking around my mother's neighborhood, gazing upon all the landscaping and gardens with beauti-

ful flowers. It helps us feel more connected when we can see what is happening around our community.

Many cities are perfect for pedestrian exploration. Walking in a busy city can be so thrilling and entertaining! Have you ever been to Manhattan? The lights, the people, the endless streets filled with shops, restaurants, art galleries, coffee houses, and everything in between can be a gratifying walking experience. Of course, with all this going on, acute awareness and observation skills are of extreme importance. Busy streets pose a completely different set of concerns that walkers need to take into consideration. Personal safety is always the number one priority.

Walking in urban areas is certainly a different kind of experience than being surrounded by Mother Nature. For some of us, it takes a vivid imagination to see all the magic and beauty in tightly nestled residential lots and manicured lawns. Despite being the confessed walker snob that I am, I occasionally find myself in less than ideal walking locations. Nonetheless, I put on the appropriate shoes and go out to discover the magic, no matter where I am.

One of my favorite affirmations is, "*I am so happy and grateful that I am always surrounded by great beauty.*" And low and behold, I always am surrounded by incredible beauty, for as we know, it is in the eye of the beholder, right? It is so beneficial to be able to shift our perspective and find the divine in everything. If you look for a captivating adventure everywhere you go, you are almost sure to find one.

Having a regular walking practice in the same location every day reveals unique gifts. I find that I form a special connection with other walkers I see regularly, produced solely because we both choose to awaken early and take a walk. I am always happy to see those people every day, and I feel as though we are friends even though we have never exchanged anything other than "Good morning!" and a smile.

> *"Between every two pines, there is*
> *a doorway to a new world."*
> —John Muir

URBAN MAGIC: THE TALE OF THE SEVEN GOLD FOXES

Whenever I think about magical walks in the city, one walk in particular sticks in my mind that I would like to share with you.

Once upon a time, I was visiting my father in my childhood town of Atlanta. He knows the magic of walking, for he would drag me out of the house for walks when I was very young and silly.

At the time, I made and sold artistic magic wands. I had made him a wand for his birthday, and we were discussing the symbols and colors I had been divinely directed to put on this particular wand. I had been instructed to use blue and lots of gold because it has such a high vibration.

One of his most powerful animal spirit guides is a fox. We were discussing the qualities of this extraordinary creature for hours that evening. We also discussed the importance of our magic numbers and how they can guide us through life experiences with profound insight. One of his "magical numbers" is seven, and he has encountered the number seven repeatedly, all over the place, throughout his life. It was a fascinating conversation and only got more interesting as we spoke further.

The next day, we went on an adventure walk, as we were accustomed to doing. We knew there was a thrilling day ahead, just waiting for us to arrive. With no particular plan, we set out in our sneakers on a chilly autumn day and began to discover the urban magic that was waiting for us, literally, around every corner.

We talked excitedly about the conversations we had had the night before as we allowed the universe to guide us down this street and that street. And just when we rounded a corner, we saw them... An installation at an art museum with SEVEN GOLD FOXES. It was a moment of pure wonderment. It was as if the universe had conspired to bring us the most astounding and synchronistic sign, we ever could have imagined that day! We both instantly knew that not only were we completely guided and supported, but that the universe has a brilliant and very shiny sense of humor! We had no doubt, magic was definitely afoot.

Our walk that day felt magical and divinely guided. We went on to be led into a Greek restaurant, met by a magnificently colorful character who proceeded to bring us Turkish coffee for a post-lunch divination reading and many other illuminating events. It was that moment in time when I watched a perfectly practical man transform into a true believer of magic... right before my very eyes!

> *"Those who don't believe in magic will never find it."*
> —Roald Dahl

BEACH MAGIC: A MEDITATION
Earthing, also called grounding, is walking barefoot on the Earth. **(More on Earthing in the chapter about FEET.)** Taking a walk on the beach is one of the easiest ways to connect to the natural healing energy that continually emanates from Mother Earth. The beach is a particularly mystical place for all the beauty and energy that exist along the edge of the Earth. It can be a place of great healing and power as the four elements converge along the shoreline.

Take a moment to visualize yourself on a beautiful sandy beach, experiencing the essence of all the elements. Take deep, long inhales and exhales as you feel the Sun upon your face, the Earth beneath your feet, the Wind whipping through your hair, and the cleansing Ocean waves lapping at your feet. The sand underneath your feet is an extraordinary mixture of Earth, crystal, volcanic rock, and crushed shells, embodying the *Earth* element. The waves crashing along the surf is the *Water* of life, expressing the intrinsic order within chaos. The element of *Air* brings the salty winds to us from the prevailing direction. The Sun, the *Fire* element, shines down, blazing the way forward, and illuminating our path.
Breathe in... Breathe out....
Hold this visualization as long as you like.

UNPLUGGING FROM DISTRACTIONS

Today, it seems we are all frequently overstimulated, and life is continuously diverting our attention elsewhere. ("Look, squirrel!") Distractions are everywhere and show up in many different forms. From incessant notifications, alerts, texts, and messages on our devices, being bombarded by advertising, fake news, commercials, to well, just about everything in between.

For many of us, it feels like a real chore to stay focused much of the time. Modern technology is truly astounding, but just like anything in life, it can become an obsession or even a severe addiction without moderation. Identifying the things in our life that are our biggest distractions can be a huge key to making successful changes. And making time to unplug from technology is one way to do this.

Distractions are covert because they are often disguised as things that seem important. Distractions can even be a subconscious self-sabotage technique blocking us from getting something meaningful accomplished While I am writing, I often get a thought that I need a cup of tea or a snack, or I need to use the bathroom, but really it's an opportunity to be vigilantly aware that potential distractions are on the prowl. I absolutely love writing this book, and yet sometimes I desperately need to go take the garbage out!

LOW-TECH TIME

In the modern quest for convenience and efficiency, we are now a predominantly technology-based society. Many people spend much of their days using computers, phones, tablets, and "smart" appliances. We are quickly losing the art of doing many things "by hand," you know, the slow way, for the sake of doing the task itself. Walking is a nearly effortless way to get back to a grounding, human-powered energy that goes way beyond bipedal locomotion.

As urban populations grow worldwide, we are increasingly an "indoor species." Along with our new sedentary ways is a whole new list of issues arising from over-consuming media on devices, causing "technostress." With stress being called the health epidemic of the 21st century by the World Health Organization, the more critical it is to find ways to alleviate it naturally. The best news is that being in nature can instantly relieve stress and help bring the whole body into a state of relaxation.

Taking a walk is a perfect opportunity to go low-tech. Taking photographs, talking on the phone, or walking with headphones while listening to music or a compelling podcast, is undoubtedly acceptable, and I do it myself. However, I highly recommend dedicating some specific time to be "device-free."

HAVE YOU HEARD OF FOREST BATHING OR *SHINRIN-YOKU*?

Shinrin-yoku means "taking in the forest through our senses," according to Dr. Qing Li, Chairman of the Japanese Society for Forest Medicine. He says that "Forest Bathing is simply being in nature, connecting with it through our sense of sight, hearing, taste, smell, and touch. Indoors, we tend to use only two senses, our eyes, and our ears. Outside is where we can smell the flowers, taste the fresh air, look at the changing colors of the trees, hear the birds singing, and feel the breeze on our skin. When we open up our senses, we begin to connect to the natural world."

What Dr. Li and most of us inherently know is that we *are* nature. We love to be outside because we are meant to be outside. And it is encoded deep within us. Being out in nature is as essential to our health as regular exercise and a nourishing diet. The next time you feel stressed or overwhelmed, I invite you to go outside and take a walk. You will find that relaxation, peacefulness, and healing is just outside your front door. For a wonderfully detailed resource all about Forest Bathing, check out Dr. Li's book, *Forest Bathing: How Trees Can Help You Find Health and Happiness.*

> **"I took a walk in the woods and**
> **came out taller than the trees."**
> —Henry David Thoreau

EVERYTHING IS A BLESSING!
Walk in awe and wonder and be grateful for every single experience that shows up. View everything as a blessing, you say? Yes! Because it is! For each and every moment conceals a remarkable gift, hidden in plain sight. If all is well, it is easy to see the blessing. But when things go amiss, there is an opportunity to behold a valuable treasure, as well. What we feel when things don't go our way is contrast.

Contrast shows us our preferences. Our beliefs about things create our preferences. When our choices are not being met, we often overlook the gift, the least of which is the freedom of acceptance. Accepting *all that is* creates inner peace, which is a way to release our resistance to life. It is our resistance that causes unhappiness.

Sadly, we are not generally taught this carefree way of existing in the world. As humans, we are often living in a constant state of unhappiness, stress, and dissatisfaction. Background anxiety can quickly become a default way of being, normalizing a life of comfortable misery. Pretty soon, nothing at all meets our expectations or satisfies our deeper needs.

So, what does all this have to do with walking? It isn't always going to be a perfect, warm, sunny day when you walk every day. Sometimes you get caught in a downpour, or a wicked cold wind picks up, or you can't find the intersecting trail you should have come upon already, or some other unfavorable circumstance. Finding the blessing in everything that happens allows us to feel more content, even when life throws a wet blanket on our picnic.

Whatever is happening isn't bad or even good. It just *is*. And when we learn to be okay with whatever just is, we are at peace. When we have this kind of peace, we are able to respond instead of mindlessly react. When we respond to life with acceptance, we soon see that nothing can negatively affect us if we do not choose to see it that way. And walks in a sudden rainstorm can be spontaneously fun and enjoyable instead of miserable. We have the power to choose, and that feels, well, very empowering!

THE NOW IS HERE
Everything is always happening in the now. The past no longer exists, and the future hasn't been written yet. Letting go of the past allows us to make room for everything new coming our way. We can respond to this moment by either remaining open

and accepting or closed and resistant. Being present is surrendering judgment. If we remain in a state of acceptance, we are free to experience the magic and the mundane all at once. One of the greatest gifts of walking in nature is how easy it is to remain in the present moment.

Fear not, for somewhere inside, we are all masters already! A shift in perspective can provide all the confirmation we need to know that anything is possible. *Embracing the Mystery* opens exciting new paths beyond our imagination and introduces unexpected wonder into everyday life. Following our intuition, the gentle and quiet whispers emanating from our hearts, and not the loud maddening voice in our heads, will lead us to the *Magic of the Wild Wood*. Here, we may catch a glimpse of these mystical wonders, lingering just around the bend.

TRAIL MAGIC

Trail Magic is a familiar expression on long-distance hiking trails, such as the Appalachian Trail. It refers to such events as finding a trail-side cooler generously packed with snacks and icy cold drinks on a hot day or even walking up on a full-on barbeque at a road crossing. I have repurposed this phrase for a far more meaningful definition of *Trail Magic* that has nothing to do with Snickers bars.

There is something inherently captivating that occurs while walking through the woods, open to the realm of spiritual illumination. Walking with sacred awareness significantly changes our experience. Our senses are heightened, our body is grounded by the Earth, and our attention to detail is remarkably enhanced. In this subtle, magical world, we are a witness to life itself, happening before our very eyes.

CAPTURING THE MAGIC WITH A CAMERA

It doesn't matter where in the world you are, they are all there, everywhere, patiently waiting for us to notice them... the secret guardians of the woods. When we remain present and aware, we can catch a glimpse into the whimsical, playful side of nature. Nature's magic is indeed alive and inviting us to come out and play.

I see something that catches my attention... What something? A flash of light, a color, a shape, a leaf, a root, a rock, a shadow on the water, a pattern in the wood, a formation of twigs, or a carved message from an ancient beetle clan. The pine beetles spend a lifetime carving intricate hieroglyphics into wood pulp, not even consciously aware of how elaborate and beautiful their dance of life is!

I snap a quick photo, sometimes two or three if I feel strongly about it. Much of the time, I don't even see what caught my attention to begin with, but a whole new menagerie of faces, magical creatures, and wood spirits- smiling, winking, and nodding at me, as if they are eager to reveal themselves. They make me laugh, usually out loud, and I know they are equally grateful for having been seen, or more accurately, *sensed*. When I see them later in the photos, I am instantaneously transported back to this whimsical world. And, I can return any time I choose, even when I am sitting at my desk, longing to be in the *Wild Wood*, once again.

> *"Align with nature...magic happens."*
> —*John Friend*

STREAM MAGIC: A MEDITATION

When you find an enjoyable place to walk in nature, with water nearby, such as a stream or a river, you have the perfect ingredients for finding *Magic in the WildWood.* With the sun shining down from above, solid Earth beneath your feet, water flowing beside you, and a gentle breeze stirring all around, you are encircled by all the elements. Here is a perfect time to take a moment to breathe deeply, fill your heart with gratitude, and allow the healing powers of all that is to seep deeply into your body.

Sit down by the edge of the water and listen to the sounds that surround you. Breathe deeply, taking long inhales and exhales. Take in the smell of the Earth, the light illuminating the sky, and the feel of the ground beneath you. In this moment, all is well. Stay as long as necessary, forgetting time for a short while.

Take this peace with you as you go about your day. You can return to it in your mind at any time to receive the medicine of all the elements of nature, just by taking a deep breath and visualizing the water, earth, air, and sun.

Chapter 3
CULTIVATING A SPIRITUAL DISCIPLINE: TRY A 40-DAY SACRED PRACTICE

Why walk?
Why Ease and Grace, of course.
They never taught us to ask for that.
Harder was somehow better,
Well, not all the time.
Hard lessons we occasionally need.
But some walks can be easy and that is just fine.
No matter what is happening out there,
Walking can inspire us to live from our best and highest self.
It is fundamental Self-Care... renewing mind, body, and spirit.
It is necessary, whole health preservation.
And walk, I must.

THE SHIFT BEGINS THE MOMENT YOU COMMIT TO IT
Walking with expanded awareness significantly changes the experience. We can bring this mystical perspective into the ordinary. Recognizing the beauty and magic of nature as it connects to your own life transforms the familiar. For it is this inspiration that is usually missing in our everyday life. There is a miraculous world out there speaking to us, patiently waiting for us to awaken.

Developing a *Sacred Practice* is enthusiastically searching for the magic in the mundane. Although only a shift in perspective, what happens is quite profound. The flowers' petals are more vibrant, the leaves on the trees are greener, and the sky appears bluer. The sudden shriek of a hawk or an enchanting encounter with a dragonfly, shimmering in the afternoon sun, carry new meaning when we focus on staying present and observing our surroundings.

Our senses come alive, and we feel the depth of grandeur that exists all around us. When we choose to see every moment as a blessing, the Earth becomes our very own cosmic playground. Every walk can be a magnificent adventure into the unknown and ceremoniously connect us to nature.

DEVELOPING A MOVEMENT PRACTICE
If you don't have a regular movement practice already, you are in for some very profound and positive changes in your life. If you already move your body regularly, then you probably already know how rewarding this habit is physically, mentally, and spiritually. And if you are just getting started, may I applaud you for your new commitment. You are in perfect time, my friend.

Now is the perfect time to start a sacred movement practice. You are ready! You can do it! No matter what age you are. No matter what size you are. No matter your current health status, there is always a place to begin on the path to healing through movement. In whatever style that calls to you, moving the body is an integral part of the journey of self-evolution.

Make it the most enjoyable experience! Experiment and find new places to explore. You will know when you find the right way because it won't feel like a chore to do it. You will want to do it. You will look forward to doing it. Your body will want to do it. And you get better and better every time you do it. And that is a most glorious feeling.

"Thinking is generally thought of as doing nothing in a pro-duction-oriented culture, and doing nothing is hard to do. It's best done by disguising it as doing something, and the something closest to doing nothing is walking."
—Rebecca Solnit

CULTIVATING A SPIRITUAL DISCIPLINE
Cultivating a Spiritual Discipline requires us to open to the mysterious divine and vigilantly remain open and willing to what flows through us. It requires inner work, commitment, and a desire to see something through to the next development, with no attachment. All the while, following our personal integrity to practice something we have no proof means anything at all. This is why it is called a Spiritual Discipline. However, that sounds pretty serious, so let's call it a Spiritual Playground instead. Couldn't we all use a little more playfulness in our lives?

If we have judgment or beliefs about experiences we may have had in the past and live life through these opinions, we often miss out on the mystery and magic in the gift of the *now*. The way we perceive things we may have learned in the past may not have been right for us then. Be open to the possibility that we just weren't ready yet. The Universe is continually inviting us to have new experiences. Sometimes, all we need is a new perspective.

So, with that, I recommend doing whatever feels right to you. Try whatever practices and routines that speak to you. And when you do choose to try something new, give yourself the chance to genuinely experience it. If something calls to you, choose an amount of time and days that feel like an adequate period to receive the entirety of the practice, and be open to whatever comes up. Many spiritual rituals get us quiet enough to hear hidden truths that we may not really want to hear. That is ok, too. It is all healing. Take what you want and leave the rest, and always trust your inner guidance.

TRY A 40-DAY SACRED PRACTICE

There are a lot of mysterious allegories, parables, legends, and stories around the number 40. The number has been translated into many new thought resources to mean *as long as it takes*. A *40-Day Practice* is referenced in many texts in Eastern and Western cultures. Besides being an excellent number to aim for when adding any discipline to your life, 40 days will solidify any habit you choose and give you enough time to make it your own. I suggest committing to a *40-Day Practice* to provide yourself with the best chance to make it a new exciting way of life.

DECIDE TO COMMIT

The first and most crucial step is the *decision* to make a commitment. When you decide to commit to yourself ...as opposed to think it over, consternate, sit on the fence, mull it over... the Universe responds immediately, and things begin to shift. The Universe literally *wants* you to succeed and helps you create your ideal reality! A commitment produces creative energy and gives it a direction in which to go. I don't know about you, but that makes me feel a whole lot better!

What does it mean to you to make a commitment? The accomplishments that have meant the most to me are those that I consciously *decided* to commit to and then moved forward without considering failure as a possibility. There was no doubt in my mind; I was fully committed.

Now, for an experiment, I am inviting *you* to think of a significant accomplishment in your life, something that made you proud of yourself. Do you remember the commitment you made when you began? When we just want something, it is one thing ...meh... and then, there is sincerely committing. Was it just dumb luck that you achieved what you did? Or, did you decide *to make the commitment* to yourself and accept nothing less? The difference is stark.

When we observe those who have achieved success, the dominant characteristic is the *resolve* to succeed. Commitments are powerful because they affect how you respond to life, no matter what is happening around you. You work harder to achieve, look for ways around the inevitable obstacles, and you never see quitting as an option.

It doesn't matter if it is a personal health goal, a relationship, a career, or any other desire, the lure of quitting (and just being done with it, already!), seems to be always lurking in the background- especially on the tough days. The solution is to anticipate this phenomenon and make an agreement with yourself that you will not give up on your commitment. Energy follows a commitment. Resistance and indifference diminish when a commitment to something has been made in earnest.

"Until one is committed, there is hesitancy, the chance to draw back, always ineffectiveness. Concerning all acts of initiative or creation, there is one elementary truth...that the moment one definitely commits oneself, then Providence moves, too. All sorts of things occur to help one that would otherwise never have occurred. A whole stream of events issues from the decision, raising in one's favor all manner of incidents and meetings and material assistance which no man would have believed would have come his way. Whatever you think you can do or believe you can do, begin it. Action has magic, grace, and power in it."
—W.H. Murray (Climber in The Scottish Himalayan Expedition)

SELF-DISCIPLINE IS THE KEY TO FREEDOM

Self-Discipline does not have to be a cruel punishment. The word itself can inspire fear and dread within some. It can be a pleasurable and exciting journey of healing, inside and out. Learning to be self-disciplined is becoming more accountable to ourselves and observing how our decisions affect our minds, bodies, and spirits. Self-discipline is an evidence-based path to wholeness and freedom.

When we commit to adding a new practice to our daily routine and follow through with all the required actions to make it happen, we begin to see results. Inspired action is the most significant step following a commitment. Our efforts are validated the moment we decide a habit is worthwhile to cultivate. The results have exponential benefits as the changes that appear inspire more success as we develop self-confidence with our new practice.

Soon after beginning, a chain reaction of positive experiences begins, such as higher self-esteem, poise, and a sense of accomplishment. Sometimes it takes looking back to appreciate how far we have come. Journaling is a great way to monitor your progress, especially when you are creating new habits. You are not only adopting new behavior patterns but also rewiring your brain and building new neural pathways, called neuroplasticity.

The key is not to beat yourself up when you veer off the path. We are all human and to be human is to err. The skill is recognizing the effects of our choices and staying accountable by learning from mistakes in a loving, compassionate way. This is the path of self-care.

GUIDELINES FOR *WALKING AS A SACRED PATH*:

- **Set an intention for yourself.** It all begins with our purpose. Set realistic goals that are entirely conceivable and achievable. Evaluate what kind of health you are in and start slowly. In the beginning, it is about creating a new empowerment-building habit. It is NOT about torturing yourself by doing too much, too fast. Seriously, this is important. Ask yourself, why do you want to do this? What is your primary goal? *Most importantly, be kind to yourself.*
- **Prepare for success.** Outfit yourself with a pair of high-quality, comfortable shoes that fit your feet the best. Choose the right socks for the type of footwear you are using. What you wear on your body and feet is the most fundamental "gear" you will need, so invest in yourself. Be well-equipped by dressing appropriately and taking what you need for a safe and successful trip. (See the clothing and gear chapter for lists of the essentials.)

- **Get rid of your scale.** Or at least put it out of sight... way out of sight! If you are adding walking to your life to lose weight, please do not weigh yourself every day. Learn to use your body's intuitive sense and go by how

you feel and how your clothes fit. Our bodies can fluctuate drastically from day to day, depending on hormones,
holidays, and many other factors.

It is not fair to yourself to endlessly measure your happiness and self-worth by a scale. Happiness comes from
within. Have compassion and self-discipline, and the
weight will naturally come off. Obsessing over numbers
never heals the emotional wounds that cause extra
weight in the first place.

- **Have a plan.** Know where you are going when you walk
  out the door. Have a general route in mind and tell someone where you are going. There are tons of great apps for
  smartphones these days. Some are pedometer apps,
  while others have many more capabilities, so do a little
  research. Using a pedometer can be very motivational. I
  know several people that will not go to bed at night until
  they have reached their daily 10,000-steps. Now that is
  commitment!

- **Get Some Motivational Help**. Sometimes it is helpful to
  have a mentor, coach, or a walking community to keep
  us encouraged. Understanding we are not alone can
  help shift our mindset and keep us on track to reach our
  goals. Join a club or a group training program, hire a
  coach, or ask a friend for help. Find the encouragement
  you need to keep yourself feeling supported and motivated on your journey.

There really is not much you need to do. Follow the guidelines
suggested here, get help when you need it, and simply *decide to
take a walk*. Your body, mind, and spirit will thank you. So,
lace up your shoes and head outside. Explore where you live
on foot. A magnificent journey awaits you!

WALKING IS SELF-CARE

The path of Self-Care takes on a life all of its own, just like taking a walk. You naturally go where you focus. If you get distracted and look away from the path, you veer off course where you may not want to go. Life is full of one distraction after another. It can be simple things that bring us back to the center, like cultivating a spiritual practice.

If we indulge in the distractions, we may not hear the messages whispering to us by the still, small voice. Sometimes we find ourselves living in a state of numbness, making choices that are not in our best interest without being fully aware of the consequences. If we believe our stories about why we don't have what we want, we see ourselves as victims. Or, we can adopt the belief that every one of life's experiences is a real gift and be accountable for our happiness.

By accepting how powerful we are as co-creators with the Universe, we can shift from victimhood to the magnificent architects of life we are meant to be. As human beings, we are bestowed with the gifts of freedom and self-will. When we believe outside forces create our reality, we are powerless and often disappointed. Our thoughts, words, and actions today are creating our tomorrows. So, let's purposefully design an awe-inspiringly happy and inspiring life!

Self-Evolution is not for sissies. It is the path of choosing self-love first and learning to recognize what that means for us as individuals. It is setting an intention to create a self-disciplined life in a way that is fun and meaningful. Walking can do that for us.

Transformation can simply be making tiny changes in our thoughts, beliefs, and actions. A new perspective can transport us out of stagnant thinking and into a fresh and invigorating existence. Visualize yourself awakening to a new ideal way of living. If you get the thought to try something new, do not lose the momentum that is already stirring within. Whatever *inspired action* is calling you, do it! I am inviting you to own it. I mean, really OWN IT. Just decide and do it. Whatever it is. BE AMAZING!!!! Be an authentic, badass You.

"Action breeds confidence and courage. If you want to conquer fear, do not sit at home and think about it. Go out and get busy."
—Dale Carnegie

Chapter 4
OTHER SACRED PRACTICES

How does one increase their Awareness?
Meditation.
What is meditation?
It is nothing.
There are many different kinds,
and this is another one:
Surrender to life and open your senses!
Smell the poignant aroma of the sweet cedar...
Feel the subtle liveliness of a crisp fall day...
Taste the salty air of the noisy seashore!
Breathe and be still...
And then laugh like your life depends on it,
because it just might!

Many other Sacred Practices complement a regular walking routine. When performed together, these spiritual disciplines provide a system of whole health, stimulating self-transformation physically, mentally, emotionally, and spiritually.

ANYTHING CAN BE A SACRED PRACTICE

Some would call only specific spiritual disciplines a *Sacred Practice*, such as yoga, meditation, or other rituals. But in reality, any activity can become a *Sacred Practice*. By observing an ordinary task as a *Sacred Practice*, we choose to see the activity as a Self-Care ritual and a way to connect with the Divine. A subtle yet powerful shift takes place within us that summons our "Higher Self" with our conscious mind and body, even while performing rather mundane tasks.

As we walk down the path of Awakening, we can embrace other daily rituals as *Sacred Practices*. Some examples are sending loving thoughts to your teeth and gums while brushing and flossing them. Repeat thoughts like, "I have bright, healthy, straight teeth and healthy gums." Or, "I love my teeth!" I am not joking when I say that my teeth are in the best shape they have ever seen!

Blessing our food is nothing new, but we can revitalize rote traditions with vibrant new energy. As I hold my hands over my food, I am filled with gratitude, and I visualize sending healing power going into the food, knowing it is wholly nourishing my body when I eat it. You can do this with any routine endeavor, such as before drinking water, taking supplements or medication, or even bathing. Be creative! There is no better way to be present and aware than to remain mindful of how we accomplish our repetitive activities.

My early morning healing rituals and meditations flow into the rest of my day. Therefore, my days feel like they have an enchanted purposefulness to them. A *Sacred Practice* is taking everyday activities and imbuing them with the intention of the highest and best good. Creating a habit of living more mindfully brings so much more magic into the humdrum every day while at the same time lessening distractions. Here are some of my other favorite *Sacred Practices*...

"An early morning walk is a blessing for the whole day. "
—Henry David Thoreau

MEDITATION

There are more ways to meditate than anyone could count. When you are ready to experiment with meditation, find a practice that complements your lifestyle. In addition to moving meditations, such as *Walking as a Sacred Path*, there are an endless variety of guided meditations, sound healing, mantra chanting, Transcendental, and countless sitting meditations, such as Zen, Zazen, and the traditional ritual of simply observing the breath. With the right mentality, folding laundry can be a meditation!

Meditation is the art of just being, with no attention placed on thoughts, and a full release of control. It is a practice of being the observer and letting each thought go without attachment or judgment. It is a metaphor in real-time for going with the flow while simultaneously being engaged in life. Meditation is accepting everything that happens, being only the witness, and continually coming back to the present moment.

Some people find it easier to learn the power of meditation through movement better than stillness. This meditation style is the essence of *Walking as a Sacred Path.* If you have difficulty sitting still, this might be a revolutionary new tool! Everything we believe, we have the power to change. It is not our DNA that solely programs us, but the focus we place on the choice in each moment. Whatever we focus on becomes a habit until there is an intentional redirection.

WHAT DOES MEDITATION DO?
Meditation and prayer raise our vibrational frequencies, strengthen our intuition, and support our connection to our divine nature. Meditation is a fundamental tool in developing a spiritual practice of any kind. Like anything we wish to learn, a new approach takes time to develop. The benefits of quieting the mind and being present have infinite value in every aspect of our lives. Meditation allows us to make everyday decisions from a place of peace and helps maintain tranquility amidst the storms.

Because our thoughts can move and direct energy, meditation is instrumental for personal transformation. When we practice surrendering to life, we open a channel of divine guidance that leads to peace. Meditation practices provide sacred space to hear intuitive messages and inner knowing. When we ask, if we are willing and open, the answers will come.

YOGA
The word *yoga* means "to unite," as in, to unite mind, body, and spirit. Yoga is not just a set of physical postures, called asanas, but a system for a whole way of *being*. There are many different kinds of yoga. There is even "Laughter Yoga," which, of course, is one of my favorites, but any yoga is hugely beneficial. There is a style of yoga for every individual and body type.

I believe that a yoga practice is one of the best counterparts to a regular walking routine. On a purely physical level, the movements augment each other so effectively, it is as if they are designed to go together. Yoga aligns and stretches the whole body, keeping the entire system functionally balanced. After going for a long walk, my body loves nothing more than gentle yoga stretches.

The more full-body movement we do, the more full-range long-term motion we will maintain. You know the old saying, "Use it or lose it"? Well, that is pretty much how it works. Walking is the best movement we can do for our bodies, and gentle stretches will enhance that motion all the more.

Stretching, such as yoga asanas, helps muscles recover more quickly and expands your range of motion. Yoga improves your balance, agility, and flexibility, which come in handy for activities that require moving quickly, such as rock-hopping across a creek, or, avoiding obstacles in your path.

Feeling flexible and balanced are central to having self-confidence on the trail, as well as the sidewalk. Being able to respond quickly to variable terrain is a skill that is learned by experience. A sense of balance occurs mostly in the brain and is directly associated with your beliefs. If you believe you can do it, you can! So, giving yourself the time to practice will ensure that you are quick on your feet and positively upright.

Along with walking, yoga is one of the best moving meditations, allowing the participant to focus on the movement itself. Experiment with different styles until you find one that resonates with your lifestyle. Start by learning an easy, basic set of asanas and make it part of your daily routine. "Practice makes perfect," and the results can be truly remarkable.

THE FOUNTAIN OF YOUTH: THE 5 TIBETAN RITES
The Five Tibetan Rites are five simple yogic movements that have been regularly described as nothing less than the "Fountain of Youth." When the exercises are performed daily as a *Spiritual Discipline*, they can greatly assist with personal development-physically, mentally, and spiritually. Because our thoughts and actions physically alter our body and brain, these relaxed postures can have a profound effect when implemented regularly.

Peter Kelder, the author of the book, *Ancient Secret of the Fountain of Youth,* explains how these five exercises balance and regulate the body's seven chakras, or energy centers, which govern the endocrine system. He maintains that the rites help reclaim youth and vitality by restoring these vortices of energy to their proper speed and direction of spinning. Kelder instructs the reader to perform each rite three times daily, gradually increasing the repetitions until performing each rite 21 times. It is a straightforward daily practice and takes less than 10 minutes to complete all five for the prescribed number of repetitions.

The book is filled with reports of miraculous accomplishments and fascinatingly mysterious accounts. At the time of this writing, I have been doing the rites daily for over five years. I do them first thing in the morning before any of my other meditations. I can honestly say I could write an entire book on the benefits I have experienced by adding these to my daily rituals. I highly recommend them!

DANCING: SACRED MOVEMENT

The word dance is often misinterpreted, instilling a sense of sudden uncomfortable fear instead of a symbol of pure joy and freedom. Instead, I like to call it *Sacred Movement* because it is action that happens through us, not from us. *Sacred Movement* is allowing our bodies the space to express the creative energy that naturally dwells within us. This form of personal expression feels particularly important in times of extreme emotion, be it positive or negative.

Like leaves on a tree gracefully moving in a breeze, *Sacred Movement* through dance is natural and vital to all of life. A powerful tool for awakening subtle energies within us, it is an outer expression of our inner Spirit. It is not a performance; it is whole-body participation. There is not a right or wrong way to do it. *Sacred Movement* allows us to transcend our state of mind and reach higher states of consciousness.

A celebration of life, dancing awakens the primal force within us that responds to the rhythm of the Universe. Almost like a cleansing prayer, freedom of movement allows us to express healing, grieving, and joy in a way that is ancient and universal. However, the music we listen to has a significant impact on us consciously and subconsciously. I recommend listening only to uplifting music or songs with positive, inspiring messages.

JOURNALING: WRITE IT DOWN!
Be your own witness. Do you write in a journal? If so, you probably already know how incredibly insightful this habit can be. If not, hopefully, you soon will know the wonders of this simple practice. All I have to do is go back and read entries from the past to see how far I have come! I view it as an intuitive healing process to release thoughts, concerns, hopes, and whatever comes up to the paper.

In the process of self-transformation, recording our thoughts and beliefs about what is happening in our lives can be very empowering. Free-form writing is a great way to release stored up emotions as well as record important milestones. It is a precious tool that can be a daily custom simply by keeping a journal and a pen beside your bed or favorite chair.

A fun, creative writing exercise is to write down in detail all the what's and why's of your biggest goal or dream to have a solid understanding of what you want to create in your life. Writing our desires down on paper is the first step in magical manifestation (especially right before a new moon). You don't need to figure out the how's, as this is the part the Universe likes to make up. All we have to figure out is what we want and ask for it! Spend some time writing, stream-of-consciousness-style (without too much thought), and then let it go. It is often very illuminating to go back later and see what you wrote.

Still not convinced journaling is the best thing since sliced bread? Well, let me share a little tale with you. A few years ago, in one of my many moves, I was unpacking a box of books and journals. As was my habit, I was flipping through some old journals I hadn't seen in a while and came across one that caught my attention. I found a list on the back page of things I wanted to manifest. I was absolutely astonished when I realized I had accomplished everything on the list! And these were big things, such as start my own business, plant a garden, lose 100 pounds, and hike the Appalachian Trail. Everything on that list I had successfully completed in the 11 years between writing it down and reading it on that auspicious day. Journaling works wonders for sending out into the Universe exactly what you want, as well as releasing all that no longer serves you. It is a profound tool and will always be in my repertoire of daily rituals.

PLAYING: IT'S NOT JUST FOR KIDS
Somehow, we have acquired the notion that life is supposed to be serious. And there are certainly times when seriousness is appropriate. But it is most definitely not all the time, even though I find myself slipping back into it without much effort. However, incorporating a whimsical perspective of *play* brings levity and new, light energy to the often gloomy, doomsday world we hear about on the evening news. So, go dress up as your favorite character and sing out of key at the top of your lungs, or whatever makes you cackle at the mere thought of doing it, and play. (Or just have some kind, any kind, of fun, for goodness sake!)

Once upon a time came the "seriousness movement" that successfully embedded the belief that "playing" is just for children. Well, I am here to proclaim, this movement is counterproductive and downright injurious for happy humans of all ages. Being playful and laughing is one of the best behaviors we can adopt for optimum health. Seriously! (Pun intended.) My daily walks feel like "playing" because I am always pretending (not really) that I am in an enchanted forest (they all are) looking for magic (which is everywhere)!

What do you do that feels like playing? Ok, well, go do some of THAT!

LAUGHTER YOGA: IT'S A THING!
So, you want to take this *play* concept a little further? You are officially being given permission to be ridiculously silly and laugh at whatever you want, anytime, for absolutely no reason at all. Whew! What a relief, because life can feel so serious! Knowing the difference between acting "childish" and "child-like" makes all the difference. To feel we have permission to be as children- present, innocent, and perfectly in the moment- is liberating and most definitely a *Sacred Practice*.

It is funny to me that the old familiar sayings such as, "Laughter is the best medicine," seem to be the truest and yet, most under-appreciated. There is a comprehensive and medically verified list of positive, healing effects that laughter has on the human body. The most sincerely beneficial things are the most basic tenets of life, most of which we take for granted. What about the possibility that everything we need to know we instinctively knew how to do when we were infants, such as eat, drink, breathe, play, dance, poop, smile, love, and laugh? So, go on now, what are you waiting for? Have yourself a good little chuckle, for no reason at all, before you go about with your day. Hehe.

SMILES ARE GOLDEN: "GOOD STUFF SPREADS TOO!"
Ok, maybe you aren't quite ready to find out where the spontaneous fits of "out loud laughter" can take you, but here's one you can probably pull off, how about *Smiling* as a *Sacred Practice*?

Did you know that smiling is one of the most valuable and yet one of the easiest gifts you can give? When I am walking, I make it a point to smile at every person I see because I know that a smile can mean so much and is so easy to give. And it makes me feel good to smile at people. I have had many experiences where something positive happened just because of a simple smile. Smiles are so incredibly underrated!

Smiling is beautiful because it is beneficial to the receiver as well as the giver. Because it is impossible to genuinely smile while angry or frustrated, it is a surefire way to lift your spirits. When you smile, you release feel-good hormones in your body, and therefore, it instantly raises your vibration. This means that whenever you smile, you begin to feel better instanta-neously. It is the quickest and most effective healing technique you could ever imagine for others and yourself. Just like laugh-ter, a smile is contagious. Let's spread some love and share a smile with everyone! "Good stuff spreads too!"

DIVINE EXPERIMENTATION...
Whether it's walking, meditation, or fits of spontaneous laugh-ter, I invite you to experience any new ritual with fresh eyes. Sometimes we receive immediate benefits, and other times it takes months or even longer to see the subtle effects. Take a chance and view life as an opportunity to be in the whimsical hands of divine order. Having a playful, curious attitude will reveal a much richer experience than reluctantly giving some-thing minimal effort.

Being an *Experimentalist* is the ceaseless trying of new things, playing with ideas, finding our edge, and sampling life like a de-lectable buffet. When we search to find the hidden passions that we have yet to discover and keep our eyes open for oppor-tunities that pique our interest, we find them in not-so-secret places. It is never too late to learn anything. It is the "divine discontentment" that keeps us seeking and exploring, ad infinitum. Until... we need to seek no longer. When we find ourselves in the void of the unfulfilled and unknown dream, it becomes known. And then it becomes familiar. And then, it becomes a passion! Try something new and exciting just to see what happens!

Chapter 5
BE A *KEEPER OF THE LAND:*
WALKING & HIKING ETIQUETTE

Why walk?
This mountainside, mossy, gurgling creek trail is exactly what my
spirit craves.
The deep musky smells and the perpetual sound of trickling water.
And just now, I spot the beautiful spherical red fruit peeking out
from the trillium leaves.
I witnessed it.
I was here at the moment of fruitfulness.
Life, in action.
I am now a part of this experience.
Just as the ancient Hawaiian mantra, Ho'oponopono, teaches;
I love you, I am sorry, please forgive me, thank you.
We are ALL of this.
When I walk, I can hear the sunshine playing upon the rocks in a
dappling dazzling dance.
I can feel the chirping and singing and calling from lofty perches.
The breeze beckons me outside
with the anticipation of refreshing my deepest hopes and dreams
How could I not do this?

BE A *KEEPER OF THE LAND*

Being a *Keeper of the Land* is loving and caring for our wild, outdoor spaces as if they are our own. To be a dedicated advocate for nature is to see the world around us as *an extension* of ourselves. We are the most advanced species on the planet (or so we think), and with that knowledge comes an inherent responsibility to care for the Earth. This could be adopting a more compassionate attitude, joining and donating to nature-preservation focused charitable organizations, or learning and teaching conservation techniques to others.

Beyond just picking up litter found along the trail and following the standard *Leave No Trace* Principles, being a good steward of the environment is opening to a deep connection with *all that is*, seen and unseen. For as above, so below, and so within, so without. How we treat the outside world is how we treat our inner world. The state of each reflects the beliefs and behavior patterns we hold about ourselves and all others. There is no belief system necessary to sense this innate connection we all share. It dwells within all things.

It is easier to get cozy with the notion that we are a part of nature if we have a fundamental understanding that we are all just energy. We are all vibrating to the frequency that we *choose* to tune into, just like a radio station. We choose frequencies to tune into by focusing on them, whether we do this consciously or not.

This phenomenon is also called the "Law of Attraction," which essentially states that "like attracts like." So, if we walk into the forest with the understanding that we are a part of this landscape, part of the weather, part of this Earth... we are present for life itself, in every way possible. We are giving our full attention while at the same time, fully receiving.

And receive we do! As we walk among the trees, wildflowers, meadow grasses, or sand dunes, we welcome this abundant gift with every cell in our body. It changes everything around us. And we are forever changed as we grow and learn and adapt to our surroundings with divine surrender. Let the path, road, or trail carry you to your destiny with every step. Own it. You are a walker on a sacred path.

We have forgotten how to be good guests, how to walk lightly on the earth as its other creatures do.
—Barbara Ward

WALKING AND HIKING ETIQUETTE

For me, being in the woods is to witness nature as a Sacred Sanctuary. When I step into a forest, a tremendous peace begins to come over me. As I take in the sounds of birds singing, squirrels rustling about, or the wind rustling in the leaves of the trees, I feel a calm envelop me like a soft sigh of relief.

Walking into the forest as if you are entering a tranquil, holy place can reveal a much more profound experience. Awareness is a fundamental aspect of respect, safety, and the essence of the experience itself. Watching, observing, and adapting to all that surrounds you, can be a powerful Spiritual Practice. Having a deep respect for the land as a sacred place is a magnificent place to begin.

The good news is that cultivating consciousness of our surroundings is a habit we can foster, just like planning for a variety of unforeseen happenings. What are the potential issues around the outing you are organizing? Proper planning and preparation include considerations such as the weather, altitude, topography, wildlife, and the individuals' health and abilities in the group. It is essential to have the skills and knowledge to handle the most likely situations you will encounter and gives you the confidence to enjoy your ventures with peace of mind.

When I began to write this section, I realized every one of the guidelines of "Hiking Etiquette" that I felt it necessary to discuss could be found in at least one of the "Leave No Trace" (LNT) seven principles. The benefit is that these "rules" for caring for the land are easy to understand and follow so that everyone gets to enjoy these special places.

Our public lands are here for everyone to enjoy. With education and mindfulness, we can all do our part to keep our sacred natural places wild and safe for everybody. Here are the official guidelines that have been extrapolated from my Leave No Trace Certification training and the official guide, "*Leave No Trace in the Outdoors*" by Jeffrey Marion, Ph.D.

> **"Take nothing but pictures, leave nothing but footprints,**
> **kill nothing but time."**
> —Aliyyah Eniath

WHAT IS "LEAVE NO TRACE," ANYWAY?
The Leave No Trace Center for Outdoor Ethics is an educational nonprofit organization devoted to responsible recreation and active stewardship of the outdoors. LNT was officially born in 1994 by federal land management agencies and the National Outdoor Leadership School (NOLS) to develop and promote low-impact outdoor skills and ethics. These are necessary to protect the ecological and experiential health of all our outdoor environments.

LNT consists of seven core principles to provide education, knowledge, and awareness of the adverse effects of recreational impact. The best way to learn them is to practice them. The best way to practice them is to teach them. So, please remember these basic concepts and share them with your friends, family, and hiking buddies to preserve the beauty of our natural resources for generations to come. It is all of our responsibility to create the best and safest adventures possible.

LEAVE NO TRACE SEVEN PRINCIPLES:
- Plan ahead and prepare
- Travel and camp on durable surfaces
- Dispose of waste properly
- Leave what you find
- Minimize campfire impacts
- Respect wildlife
- Be considerate of other visitors

1. PLAN AHEAD AND PREPARE
Outdoor knowledge and skills are essential elements of safe, outdoor fun. Skills will vary significantly by setting, activity, and season. Poor planning and preparation can turn a leisurely hike into a potentially dangerous situation.

Today, it is easy to do a little internet research and determine what rules or regulations apply to certain areas. Many trails, for example, cross private property. Knowing whether camping is permitted, local fishing regulations, the maximum number allowed in groups, pet-leash laws, and where to park are just a few examples.

Each area has its own set of specific hazards. Planning includes understanding the terrain and what gear and clothing you may need. Anticipate problems such as emergency extraction due to injury or illness, unforeseen changes in weather, poorly marked trails, flooded creek crossings, or any variety of unexpected events.

Planning and preparing make for a more peaceful event for the entire group. Organizing smaller groups helps reduce trail erosion and lessen the overall destruction of the surrounding terrain. Emergency rescue scenarios can be some of the most dangerous and the most damaging activities for the environment.

Planning and preparing include having all the essentials for the particular outing you plan for safety and having fun. Always have a map and compass, pertinent information about the area where you will be, as well as knowledge and skills about how to use these tools. Understanding the first principle is the most critical step because we have all the resources at hand *before arriving at the trailhead* to ensure a safe and successful trip.

2. TRAVEL AND CAMP ON DURABLE SURFACES

Trampling sensitive vegetation only takes a moment, where recovery from this impact can take years. Durable surfaces include rock, gravel, snow or ice, barren soils, pavement, and well-established trails and recreation sites. Preserve native vegetation by not stepping on plants and avoid creating new barren areas.

Stay on well-established trails and especially avoid expanding these areas. So, what does this mean when you come upon a mud puddle? That's right! It is best to walk right through it to prevent damage to sensitive vegetation along the sides of the trail. So, wear durable waterproof shoes, boots, or gaiters and have some fun splashing through those muddy spots!

Recovery rates of some impacted areas can require ten to thirty years to recover! Please do not venture off-trail. A shortcut on a switchback can severely damage a delicate ecosystem. Informal trail networks disrupt wildlife habitats, hasten the dispersal of non-native plants, and degrade very quickly because of erosion. There is also the possibility of getting lost or confused because the trail is not on the map.

"A nation that destroys its soils destroys itself. Forests are the lungs of our land, purifying the air and giving fresh strength to our people."
—Franklin D. Roosevelt

3. DISPOSE OF WASTE PROPERLY: "Pack it in, Pack it out!"
Did you know that even leaving just a few food crumbs is sufficient to attract wild animals? This can have a devastating impact on wild animals and future visitors. Bears can quickly develop nuisance behavior by losing their fear of humans through exposure to human food. ***Never feed wildlife.***

It is also not healthy to give wild animals human food. They need to eat what they are supposed to eat, and your Cheetos probably isn't in their preferred diet. I know it is so tempting, and we think we are helping them, but they need to remain self-sufficient by finding their own food.

Have you heard the phrase, "Pack it in, Pack it out?" Being a responsible *Keeper of the Land* is picking up ALL the garbage you find along the trail and around your picnic spot (that you can comfortably carry, of course). I always have a couple of plastic bags to pack out what I find along my walk. The habit of leaving a place "better than I found it" has become not only a regular custom for me but also an activity that brings me great joy.

NOT JUST LITTER, BUT ALL WASTE!
Believe it or not, the orange peels and apple cores are just as important to pack out. Not only is it unsightly to come across someone's tossed banana peel, but it can attract wildlife. It is inappropriate to bury food or trash and never attempt to burn it. You can never completely burn food, and buried food is easily found and dug up. If you carry it into the woods, please bring it home with you, too.

It is an important habit to check any area where you have spent time, such as taking a break on the side of a trail or after camping, for personal items, garbage, and food scraps as well. A "final sweep" is an ideal habit to develop and might uncover essential forgotten things that you may be frantically looking for later. It only takes a few seconds but can save yourself a big headache and much wasted time!

HUMAN WASTE: SO, HOW DO YOU POOP IN THE WOODS?
Ahh, let's address the age-old question, "How do you poop in the woods??" Well, as you might imagine, there is a right way and, well, every other way. Nobody likes to stumble upon anybody's poop in the woods. Or, for that matter, see toilet paper flowers behind trees. So, let's get this down correctly, friends.

Below the tree line, where there is plenty of organic matter and topsoil, it is proper to dig a "cat-hole." Using a small trowel, dig a hole 6-8" deep and 4-6" wide at least 200' (generally around 70-80 steps) from water, campsites, and trails. After the waste is in the hole, cover and disguise the area thoroughly with dirt and leaves. (By the way, the trowel only touches dirt!)

Biodegradable unscented toilet paper is fine to bury in the hole, but always pack out wipes, diapers, or feminine hygiene products because these items contain microplastics that decompose very slowly. The best method is to disperse cat-holes throughout the day on a hike so that there is no high concentration near any water source or campsite.

Above the tree line, where there is little or no topsoil, it is proper to pack out all human waste and toilet paper. Slickrock areas, river canyons, deserts, or areas with permafrost are unique environments where human waste has a higher probability of polluting waterways. It will not decompose readily because of the extreme weather conditions. Many land managers in these and other areas require visitors to carry out human waste in a bag, sometimes called a "wag bag." This method is particularly important in environments where it is difficult or impossible to dig a proper cat-hole.

Urine is not typically a problem. Avoid concentrated noxious urine smells by dispersing it, so it does not damage plants or aquatic life by urea salts, ammonia byproducts, and excessive nutrients. It is imperative to maintain a 200' buffer away from water sources for urine, too.

YEP, PACK OUT SPOT'S POOP, TOO!

Pet waste is an increasing problem and can pose health concerns to you, children, wildlife, and other pets. Diseases and parasites can be easily transmitted by exposure. It is best to carry a bag and pick up all pet waste or use the same methods for disposing of human waste. That moment when you realize you have just stepped in dog poop (or worse, human poop!) doesn't make for the best outdoor memories. Please be considerate of others.

4. LEAVE WHAT YOU FIND

"Leave only your footprints" is a standard LNT message you may have already heard. Take photographs, observe, and learn all about the area you are visiting, but leave what you find so others may experience it, too. If we pick the wildflowers, remove native wildlife, or collect archeological artifacts to keep as souvenirs, others do not have the same experience. Numerous studies have documented the potential harm this can cause when resources are continually removed from an area.

Practice sustainable exploration by resisting the urge to bring home keepsakes and teach others to do the same. With more and more people venturing into the outdoors, it is more important than ever to leave places as natural as possible. If you are heading to the woods to harvest mushrooms, plants, or medicinal herbs, be sure to check the appropriate land management guidelines to ensure the protection of resources. Research and apply for the applicable harvesting permits where required to do so.

LEAVING YOUR MARK IS OVERRATED!

Respect nature and leave it as you found it. A good steward does not carve on trees or other surfaces, alter natural features, or ~~even~~ create new campfire rings. Graffiti is vandalism, no matter where you are. Carving your initials into trees can introduce viruses and boring pests into the tree's inner core and quickly damage and even kill the tree.

Cairns are stacks of rocks often used as trail markers where there are few or no trees present. They are there for a purpose and should not be touched, added to, or altered in any way. Alternately, building rock cairns, anywhere else, is leaving a trace. This practice has been somewhat of a controversial subject, as some see building cairns as an art. Regardless, many people do not want to see any sign of humankind when visiting the wilderness. We are there to experience nature in her pure and natural state. Please leave the cairn-building for private property.

"He who knows what sweets and virtues are in the ground, the waters, the plants, the heavens, and how to come at these enchantments, is the rich and royal man."
—Ralph Waldo Emerson

5. MINIMIZE CAMPFIRE IMPACTS

Although delightful on a chilly evening, there is a surprisingly long list of negative consequences of campfires. Besides the impact of campsites being utterly barren of all wood, there is extensive off-site trampling of vegetation during firewood collection. There is the unnecessary use of axes, hatchets, and saws that damage and destroy nearby trees and shrubs that are important for wildlife. There are also the trashy fire pits with half-burned logs sticking out that are unsightly to find. These needless and avoidable impacts have caused many areas to prohibit campfires altogether. If visitors learn to adopt low-impact campfire practices, maybe some of these bans can one day be lifted.

For some, having a campfire is an essential element of being outdoors. When campfires are permitted, there are some primary things to consider. Knowing if it is legal and safe to build a fire is your first responsibility. Some of the concerns are:

- What is the level of fire danger for the time of year? Is it very dry or windy conditions?
- Is there already a campfire ring, or does someone in your group know how to properly build a campfire and remove all evidence of it before you leave?
- Is there ample firewood available without denuding the entire area?
- Do you know how to properly manage a fire and extinguish it thoroughly before leaving the area?

Here are specific concerns for building campfires that Leave No Trace.

The best place to build a fire is in an existing fire ring. Build small, well-tended, manageable fires and let them burn completely to ash. Never burn trash in a fire pit because it can produce noxious fumes, smells that attract wildlife, and can leave a poisonous residue that pollutes the environment. Never leave a fire unattended and always keep wood and other fuel sources far away from fires. Put out fires with ample water, not dirt.

When gathering firewood, only choose dead and downed wood from as far away from the campsite as possible. Collect wood that is smaller than your wrist. Please keep in mind that dead and downed wood is an essential habitat for insects and other little creatures, a central food source for many birds and animals.

When extinguishing a fire, allow all wood to burn to white ash, saturate the area with plenty of water, stir it around, add more water, and stir again. Never, ever, ever leave smoldering coals behind. Fire can erupt from buried coals, and wind can pick up and carry embers up to a mile. If you are dispersed camping in a pristine site, widely scatter all *cold* ashes and any extra firewood, naturalizing the area to remove all evidence of a campfire. Like Smokey the Bear says, "Only you can prevent forest fires!"

> *"Earth provides enough to satisfy every man's needs,*
> *but not every man's greed."*
> —Mahatma Gandhi

6. RESPECT WILDLIFE:
(See Walking In Bear Country for more information.)
Observe and photograph wildlife from a safe distance to avoid startling them or compelling them to flee. Avoid loud noises, quick movements, and direct eye contact, which can be interpreted as aggression. Remember, you are a visitor in their home, and no matter what their behavior might be, they are wild and unpredictable animals. Most unwanted behavior happens when we approach too close or encroach on their feeding or mating territory.

Be particularly aware of disturbing wildlife during sensitive times such as hibernation or while foraging for food. Store all food, trash, and odorous items securely. Even stuff that is not edible to humans. Anything with an interesting smell can attract wild animals. Did I mention never feed wildlife??

Sick or wounded animals can bite, injure, or even kill you. Young animals touched by people may cause the parents to abandon them. If you come across a sick animal in trouble, please notify a game warden as soon as possible. Also, allow animals clear access to water sources by giving them a wide buffer to feel calm and secure. This consideration will minimize disruption to wildlife and ensure they have access to plenty of water.

"Our task must be to free ourselves ... by widening our circle of compassion to embrace all living creatures and the whole of nature and its beauty."
—Albert Einstein

PET SAFETY
The dog that chases wildlife not only unnecessarily stresses animals but is also in danger of being injured, diseased, or killed by a wild animal. Pets are also potential carriers and the recipients of diseases, viruses, and parasites that are often transferred through feces. As mentioned above, *please pack out all pet waste or deal with it as you would human waste.*

Many people feel that being outside in nature is an ideal time to let their dogs run free. And if you are on your private property or another person's private property with permission, this is perfectly acceptable. However, public lands are not the place to have dogs off-leash. Unleashed dogs often chase and disturb wildlife, as well as other hikers on occasion. Keeping your dog under control, on a leash, at all times is being respectful of wildlife, as well as other people.

7. BE CONSIDERATE OF OTHER VISITORS
It is becoming more critical than ever that we learn to be more considerate of others as we share trails and recreation areas. Our

public lands are subject to ever-increasing visitation levels and overcrowding, particularly at the most popular destinations. Because of our sense of freedom while spending time outside, we often disregard outdoor etiquette.

Our recreational areas must accommodate a wide variety of outdoor activities, and we must respectfully learn to share our public lands with others. If possible, plan your visits during periods of lower use and avoid the most populated destinations. Being a good steward of the environment is to remain consciously aware of how our actions affect all others.

"One touch of nature makes the whole world kin."
—William Shakespeare

SHARE THE TRAIL & BE YE KIND

Many times, it is small acts of kindness that make a big difference. Offering a friendly greeting or a smile to those you encounter, allowing others to pass, and not blocking the trail when you stop to take a break can help preserve the serenity found in nature.

Hikers going uphill always have the right of way. If you're descending a trail, mindfully step aside and allow people ascending to continue. If you approach another hiker, especially from behind, calmly announce your presence so that you are not startling them. This kind gesture also helps to keep a friendly atmosphere on the trail. If you are hiking in a group, allow others to pass by not taking up the path's entire width.

WHOSE TURN IS IT, ANYWAY?

The general rule is: Hikers yield to horses. Bikers yield to hikers and horses. Horses always have the right of way. However, if high-speed mountain bikers are coming toward you on a downhill, I would still get out of the way!

ENJOYING THE SOUNDS OF NATURE

Natural sounds, such as birds, babbling brooks, or leaves rustling in the wind, can be a healing remedy for all the stresses in life. Human-related noise can easily overpower the sounds of nature and intrude upon a peaceful experience. If you choose to listen to music, use headphones so others may enjoy the quiet of being outdoors.

Be considerate of others by using cell phones discreetly away from people. It is a perfect time to turn off the electronics and enjoy being completely present. All that being said, I love taking nature photographs. I usually keep my phone on "airplane mode" so I can still snap a quick photo.

Speak softly in the woods and avoid yelling or disturbing others with unnecessary noise, especially early in the morning or night. The discharge of firearms, barking dogs, the slamming of car doors, vehicle engines, and loud music are all common forms of noise pollution found in campgrounds and recreation areas these days. Taking care to minimize unwanted sounds and remembering that many people are enjoying nature's healing sounds will help you tune in to the natural world, too. Thank you for being a thoughtful and considerate *Keeper of the Land!*

"The earth will not continue to offer its harvest, except with faithful stewardship. We cannot say we love the land and then take steps to destroy it for use by future generations."
—Pope John Paul II

Chapter 6
THE HOW, WHERE & WITH WHOM OF IT ALL

Why walk?
Walking is our body's natural movement.
I can do many things while walking.
It can become something one does without eyes,
for the feet follow the flow of all that is.
Walking is releasing.
Releasing of all that,
whose time has come to pass.
Releasing...
Moving the life force through my entire being.
Un-stagnating.
Oxygenating all my cells.
Stimulating Mind and Body and Spirit with each new step forward.
Waking sleepy senses.
Why walk?
I must.
For I know, it is in these modest undertakings
that my most profound healing occurs.

THE NITTY GRITTY ON WALKING SAFETY:

- The number one rule is to BE SAFE. Always choose safe places to walk. If you are new to walking and hiking, locate a nearby neighborhood park or a familiar trail to visit. As your comfort level and confidence increase, your adventures will expand as well.
- Be observant of your environment. Maintain awareness of your surroundings at all times (especially if you wear headphones while you walk).
- If you choose to walk after dark, wear bright colors and reflective garments and accessories. It is advisable to have a headlamp or a flashlight and a whistle with you at all times. (Night hikes are great, especially with the aid of a bright moon. I recommend doing these with an experienced person or hiking group.)
- Walk on sidewalks where they exist, and always walk *toward* oncoming traffic. You are more visible to drivers, and you will see all approaching vehicles.
- Always tell somebody (local) what your itinerary is and when to expect your return. This courtesy gives you the confidence and freedom to explore and that others know exactly where you are.
- Be prepared for your walk by reviewing and practicing the *Leave No Trace* principles and carry all essential items needed for your specific trip.
- If you are walking in bear country, know what kind of bears there are and how to respond safely in wildlife encounters. Occasionally make noise, sing, chant, or bang your hiking poles together to prevent startling wildlife. **(Detailed information in the Walking in Bear Country section.)**

WALKING GRACEFULLY

One of the first significant achievements of a child, walking is a natural and intuitive activity. However, as we grow up, it is quite common to develop behaviors that lessen our efficiency. There are many different styles of walking that include everything from sauntering to racewalking. There is a walking style appropriate for everybody. When practicing proper technique, it matters not what manner of walking you engage in, only that you move in a way that promotes your wellbeing and balance.

It is essential to maintain a relaxed body while also feeling your inner strength and alignment with the Earth. Doing anything with a tense, anxious approach is a recipe for injury. Even when we are walking rapidly to "burn off" frustration or other heavy emotions, we can mindfully release these feelings into the ground with each step. And, in turn, draw in peaceful, relaxing energy from the Earth into our body. A simple practice before even stepping through the doorway is to visualize yourself walking with grace and ease with a big smile on your face.

> *"If I couldn't walk fast and far, I should just*
> *explode and perish."*
> —Charles Dickens

A FEW TIPS ON PROPER TECHNIQUE

Mom always told us, "Don't slouch, stand up straight!" And she was right. It is beneficial for the health of the back to maintain good posture without hunching over. Keeping the back straight is usually more challenging while ascending hills and steep grades. The body's natural response to gravity is to lean forward. By mindfully keeping the spine upright and vertically aligned, it will reduce strain on the lower back. Focus on remaining relaxed while keeping your chin neutral and parallel to the ground.

Holding your gaze upwards and not continually looking at the ground will innately help keep the body upright. If the terrain is very uneven, you will probably need to look down more often than if you are walking on a smooth surface. Having an awareness of your body position is a learned behavior. With practice, this can become a natural muscle-memory response very quickly.

Maintain a consistent stride length that is comfortable for you. When you find yourself more adept at walking, it is better for body alignment to increase your pace rather than lengthening your stride. The heel should strike the ground first, followed by the ball of the foot, and then push off with the toes and upper portion of the foot. Make your movement purposeful and walk with confidence. By keeping your body relaxed and aligned correctly with these techniques, you will be more likely to avoid injuries and preserve more efficiency with your movement.

SPEAK SOFTLY AND CARRY A BIG STICK... (OR HIKING POLES)
The movement of your arms has a significant effect on the way your body performs as well. By letting your arms swing freely in a natural arc, you are propelling yourself forward with momentum. This motion also enables the entire body to be in harmonious action while providing a total body workout. Using trekking poles engage the whole body as well. Shock-absorbing trekking poles will not only keep your arms moving in alignment with the rest of your body but can take many pounds of pressure off both knees. They are highly beneficial when carrying a heavy pack. And some of the newer lightweight tents require one or two poles for proper set-up when backpacking.

For day-hikes, I usually carry my trusted, wooden walking stick that a friend carved for me. Of course, any sturdy stick you find will do. Both poles and walking sticks are beneficial when hiking uphill by aiding with balance, having reassurance while crossing creeks, and for all kinds of safety reasons. Hidden wildlife is instantly alerted as you walk down the trail and set the stick down ahead of your footfall. Sticks and poles are also great for moving debris out of your way. In reality, they have a ton of uses... don't leave home without them!

AIM FOR 30 MINUTES PER DAY
Begin by walking slowly for a few minutes so your body can warm up and prepare for a brisker pace. If you are a beginner, start with a reasonable amount of time, such as 15 minutes a day. After this becomes a habit for at least a couple of weeks or more, slightly begin to increase your mileage and time. Start slow and celebrate all achievements, no matter how small.

When setting walking objectives, aim for a realistic goal that is conceivable and achievable to you. Something that is just out-side of your reach today, but one that feels like an accomplish-ment, will keep you motivated instead of overwhelmed. If you choose an unrealistic goal, you set yourself up for disappoint-ment that could easily wreck the whole experiment.

Perhaps make a goal to work up to a *minimum of 30 minutes of activity per day.* If you are already in good fitness, you might want to increase the time or pace. At the end of your walk, cool down by resuming a slower pace so your muscles can relax. Do some gentle stretches or yoga after your walk. If you have any health concerns, it is advisable to check with your healthcare provider before beginning any new exercise program.

> *"Everywhere is walking distance if you have the time. "*
> —Steven Wright

WALKING WITH OTHERS
Walking with friends and family is a great way to connect with other people. When I take a walk with people that I don't know very well, I inevitably make friends for life after sharing a cou-ple of hours in nature together. Because walking keeps our en-

ergy flowing, it is a great way to connect, talk through things with others, and share the exquisite splendor of being outside together. I am pretty sure that two intelligent beings on a walk can solve all the world's problems!

Hiking groups are a fabulous way to meet like-hearted friends that enjoy doing the same thing that you do. Actually, I would say it is one of the best ways to make friends... I met my first husband in a hiking group! And, of course, I am always in favor of introducing young ones to the *Magic of the WildWood.* Sometimes, it is the fun outdoor adventures and camping trips we have as children that plant the seeds for future nature-lovers and outdoor enthusiasts. I think we all need to spend more time in nature, no matter what age we are!

WALKING ALONE
All that being said, I also believe that walking alone is equally important. I frequently hike with friends, family, and clients, but for my day to day walks and hikes, I am almost always by myself. The presence of another person, anyone, regardless of your relationship, dramatically changes the nature of the walk. Without setting prior intentions and having a mutual agreement about the purpose of the walk, the energy of a "moving meditation" in nature can often be difficult to hold as a group.

Even when the group intention is "walking as a meditation," it can be challenging for some to stay present and avoid becoming distracted. I find that when I walk alone, in silence, I am much more connected to nature. The sacred space I create with each step I take upon the Earth inspires me to be a flowing force of presence.

I like walking alone because I enjoy letting nature guide me to places that catch my attention and entice me to stop, take my shoes off, and "sit a spell." Nature is magic, and I am gently guided toward the experiences calling to me when I am present and alone. When I lead others on a walk, I do not prioritize my personal preferences but allow the group to decide where and when to stop and take a rest.

IS IT SAFE TO WALK ALONE?
Many people feel that hiking alone is not safe. I wholly respect this opinion, and there are other perspectives one can explore about the subject. I believe there is no reason to be fearful about taking solitary walks in nature with the proper preparation. Before setting out alone, be adequately equipped with everything you need for the kind of hike you are undertaking, make sure you are in reasonably good health, and brush up on basic outdoor proficiency. This includes leaving your itinerary and estimated return time with somebody. Although there are inherent risks associated with any physical activity, with proper skills and preparation, you can minimize the risks and invite some genuinely extraordinary experiences into your life.

If *Walking as a Sacred Path* is your intention, I highly recommend experimenting with solitary walks, at least some of the time. You will soon notice the difference and appreciate both for the distinctive qualities they bring to the experience. However, the most important thing is just to get out and walk!

WALKING THE DOG
(See the Leave No Trace Principles for proper outdoor etiquette concerning pets.)
Dogs have been a trusted companion for many walkers and hikers. They can motivate you and help make you feel safe and protected. However, as trails get more and more crowded and our population grows along with dog ownership, it is important to address how bringing a dog affects the nature of your walk, the environment, and your relationship to others that you encounter along the way.

Bringing a dog into the wilderness can create several controversial issues. To many dog owners, these are not problems at all. The concerns are mostly about pet waste and the fact that dogs can disturb wildlife and other hikers if left to roam freely. In a nutshell, it is appropriate to keep dogs under control on a leash at all times, pick up after your pet (yes, even in the woods), and minimize the impact on others and wildlife. It is the respectful and correct thing to do.

Nevertheless, if it is a dog that will get you out of the house and walking regularly, then, by all means, go for it! Having a dog is the reason many people even take walks. The dog insists! Most dogs are just as enthusiastic about being outside as you are and need to sniff things, and pee on stuff, and well, you know. I would be remiss if I did not point out that this can significantly alter the walking experience. When possible, if you are a dog owner, add occasional solo walks to your routine as well, so you may enjoy the freedom of being outside in nature with less responsibility and distraction. Your free spirit will thank you, and Fido won't mind too much.

HOW TO FIND PEOPLE TO WALK WITH

There are many ways to find compatible walking partners. One idea is to go by your local running shoe store or outdoor outfitter and ask if they sponsor walks or hikes or know of any groups or associations that do. Often local publications will list community walking or hiking clubs. Doing a little research and asking around can lead to new ideas and remarkable friendships.

With the arrival of the internet, we now have access to endless clubs, groups, organizations, and forums. Meetup.com is a useful website and app platform that allow people to create communities specified by activity and proximity to their location. Check to see if there are any "meetups" that regularly get together and walk in your area. More populated areas will have more groups and activities from which to choose. If there isn't one that interests you, start one with your friends! There is a whole world of cool people out there that enjoy doing things you like to do.

FAMILIARITY ELIMINATES FEAR
I believe that it is one of our innate human abilities to make new circumstances, places, and people feel familiar. By searching for commonality with others, we find like-hearted people. Walking in the same area frequently makes you more comfortable with your surroundings, and stress is naturally alleviated. Familiarity builds comfort and trust.

If there is a place you wish to explore but are nervous about going on your own, bring a friend for a time or two. You will quickly become acquainted with the location and grow more relaxed each time you visit. Or, begin with a popular place on the weekend and you will never be alone, even if you wanted to be! Eventually, this will become one of your favorite places to walk because it is where you learned to embrace your power and self-confidence.

"Walking and talking are two very great pleasures, but it is a mistake to combine them. Our own noise blots out the sounds and silences of the outdoor world. The only friend to walk with is one... who so exactly shares your taste for each mood of the countryside that a glance, a halt, or at most a nudge, is enough to assure us that the pleasure is shared."
—C.S. Lewis

LET YOUR BODY CHOOSE A PLACE TO WALK
Always choose a place to walk that suits your body and present health condition by learning to trust your instincts. Our bodies fluctuate regularly, and a strenuous hike that you effortlessly

walked one day may not be appropriate for you on another day. Tuning into our bodies to see what they are asking of us is a learned habit like any other. Pushing ourselves beyond our *present* physical capabilities is a great way to throw ourselves off-course or get injured. Having awareness means developing our observation skills and also inquiring within to sense the next right move.

I choose a location to walk based on considerations such as the weather, how much time I have, how my body feels that day, and other relevant factors. I pick a destination by intuition, common sense, and little scrutiny from my mind. Surrendering to life includes deciding where I go for a walk.

NO, REALLY, WHERE SHOULD I WALK?
Whether you are a beachcomber, an urban wanderer, or a mountain hiker, there is almost always a place to walk relatively close. Start with where you live. Inspire your sense of curiosity. If you have a safe neighborhood, road, trail, or beach nearby, you are in luck! If you are an avid adventurer like me, try exploring different areas and see which appeal to you the most.

Do you have any parks nearby that have walking trails? If you are lucky enough to live near forested nature trails, I highly recommend investigating all your options to find your favorites. If you walk the same path over and over again, you learn to find interesting things hidden in plain sight. No matter how many times I hike a trail, I always see something I have never seen before. This practice continually expands my observation skills to find new things in familiar, well-known places and keeps me from getting bored. The old cliché is real; it is all about the journey and rarely about the ultimate destination.

ASK FOR A NICE PLACE TO WALK, AND YOU SHALL HAVE IT!
My requirement for living anywhere is that I can walk out the door and go for a walk. I established this "personal rule" early

in my walking days. I lived on a scary, busy road with no shoulder and nowhere to walk. This dissatisfaction was the catalyst to move to a new place where I found a super magical place to wander!

I now simply ask to be guided to enchanted places to walk, and they always appear. I begin by expressing my gratitude for a safe and rewarding adventure and then follow my intuition. If I hear mention of a trail repeatedly, or I suddenly get an idea, I act on it. Being the perennial nomad, I now find myself walking in the most amazing places I could ever dream up. Allow divine guidance to spark *inspired action*!

DIFFERENT TYPES OF TRAILS, PATHS, & TERRAIN

THE BENEFITS OF WALKING OFF-PAVEMENT

Besides being in a beautiful place, such as a path through enchanted woods or along a shimmering beach, there are many benefits to walking on uneven terrain. The most profound advantage is a whole-body experience. Having walked many miles on pavement and dirt, I have noticed more apparent differences, and then there are the more subtle.

When I am walking directly on the Earth, I feel more deeply connected. Even with rubber-soled footwear, I can feel each stride settle on the dirt, moss, or leaves. Leaping from rock to rock through a creek becomes a spirited game, filled with child-like wonder. This intimate connection with our planet is a phenomenon that must be experienced to grasp fully. The ground below the feet feels infinite, untouched by the hand of man, primordial and deeply healing.

There are substantial physical benefits, as well. Walking on uneven terrain triggers many small physiological changes to take place within the body. Many different muscles, ligaments, and tendons are activated and stimulated when walking over roots and rocks. The body's core is working efficiently to maintain balance as you subconsciously make rapid decisions about where to place the next footstep. We are more often present and engaged as we focus on where to find the most stable footing. *I believe walking on uneven terrain, along with regular stretching practices such as yoga and dancing, are the best activities you can do to increase balance, flexibility, and agility.*

WALKING ON SIDEWALKS & OTHER FLAT SURFACES
There are benefits to walking down the street on a sidewalk or a paved trail, too. Flat surfaces are safer for those that have poor balance, vision, or vertigo issues. There are usually fewer tripping hazards, so it can be much smoother, especially when beginning a new practice. When walking on flat surfaces, many people are able to sustain a quicker pace.

This faster-paced walking style is an excellent choice for cardiovascular training, rather than meandering slowly down a dirt path, taking carefully chosen steps. You will probably cover more miles and steps by the uninterrupted pace you can reach while quickly moving across a smooth surface. Concrete or paved surfaces can be harder on the joints, however. Proper footwear can help cushion the repetitive pounding steps taken on hard surfaces.

LOOP TRAILS
Loop trails are great because there is no point you must turn around and retrace your steps. You are always going in the right direction to get back to where you started, and every moment is new scenery. If you walk a loop trail, I recommend experimenting with it in both directions. You will most likely find that it is an entirely different experience going in the opposite direction. In mountainous terrain, it is usually more physically demanding in one direction than the other. On popular

trails, you might find that one direction feels less crowded than the other because most people are going the other way.

OUT-AND-BACKS

An out-and-back is walking a route to a certain point of interest or mile marker and then turning around and returning to where you started. Like going "backward" in a loop, the trail is entirely different in the opposite direction. You see things you can't believe you missed going the other way.

Some hikers tend to be very destination-oriented, and therefore in a constant state of anticipation for an end goal. If your intention is *Walking as a Sacred Path,* every moment brings joy, and the waterfall or vista at the end is just icing on the cake. By genuinely appreciating each step along the way, we feel more fulfilled by the end of the journey, no matter how far along the path you get.

LABYRINTHS: SACRED MOVING MEDITATION

A labyrinth is an ancient, twisting pathway, with only one route to the center that forms a pattern within a circle. Labyrinths have been utilized for centuries as a sacred space for moving meditations and self-reflection. Many people see walking the maze to the center and back out again as a journey to our center and back out into the world again. Whatever way you view this special walking meditation, it can be a unique way to experience *Walking as a Sacred Path.* Find one near you at www.labyrinthlocator.com.

EARTHING...THE HEALING MAGIC OF WALKING BAREFOOT

Although human beings began wearing shoes approximately 40,000 years ago, it has been perpetually understood that to walk on the Earth, making physical contact with the ground, has significant health benefits. Walking barefoot is one of the most healing and grounding (literally) things we can do for our body, physically, mentally, and spiritually.

"Forget not that the earth delights to feel your bare feet and the winds long to play with your hair."
—Khalil Gibran

Earthing, also called Grounding, is the practice of making contact with the electrons on the Earth's surface and receiving this regenerative energy by walking, sitting, or laying on the ground. However, because we spend such a disproportionate amount of time walking around with insulated soles on our shoes and living inside buildings, we are disconnected from this vital energy source. Many people feel this is a significant contributing factor in the continuous rise of chronic disease.

Scientific research supports that Earthing has measurable benefits such as reduced pain and inflammation and improved sleep by balancing circadian rhythms. Walking barefoot alleviates anxiety and stress, which helps strengthen the immune system. Of course, anytime we are in nature, we naturally become more energized. Earthing can also reduce the accumulated electromagnetic charge within the body by absorbing negative electrons directly from the Earth.

However, before you toss all your shoes, there are some challenges to moving toward a barefoot walking practice. Because of the general disconnect we have on the Earth, many people are quite tender-footed and unable to walk great distances barefoot. Have you ever gone to the beach on vacation and walked too far, too fast? If you are not used to being barefoot, it is easy to enflame tender skin, even on the calloused bottoms of your feet. Prolonged barefoot walking in sand or other soft surfaces can also cause the soft tissue to become aggravated and cause plantar fasciitis, a painful foot condition.

Any ritual we can incorporate that reconnects us to the Earth, whether it is walking directly on the Earth's surface or merely sitting or lying on the ground, will have numerous positive effects. As with any new practice, it is best to start with a short amount of time and allow your body to adjust to walking barefoot slowly. Be sure to choose clean, safe locations, free from sharp objects, pet waste, or other dangerous hazards. Earthing could be a delightful addition to any meditation or a warmup for a sacred walking practice.

"Barefoot travel allows you to get the true feel of a place."
—Sabrina Ward Harrison

LEARNING TO FLOW LIKE WATER: A MEDITATION
Begin with long, deep inhales and exhales. Close your eyes as you visualize walking briskly down a beautiful path. You arrive at a small stream with perfectly positioned stepping stones to cross the water safely. You hop from one to the other with childlike enthusiasm and skillful grace. You laugh out loud often during your thrilling adventure. You deftly move down the path feeling strong and confident. You are flowing, in perfect harmony, just like the water in the stream. Breathe in... Breathe out...

As you flow up and down a trail like a rivulet of water, bounding from rock to root, as if you are dancing upon the surface, you feel more and more relaxed and comfortable on uneven land. With repetition, it can be surprising how quickly you feel agile, flexible, and balanced. Visualize yourself bounding from one stone to the next, having a deep inner sense of knowing that you are protected, guided, and proficient in this activity.

In the physical plane, with regular practice comes grace, ease, and self-confidence. It is a fun challenge of inner trust, to believe you are becoming more and more balanced on your feet, with almost immediate and noticeable results. The practice of visualizing being a responsive, stable walker helps us to trust ourselves in all of life's situations. This exercise yields excellent outcomes over time. Repeat it often!

Chapter 7
WHAT SHOULD I BRING WITH ME?

Why walk?
Well, to slow down, of course.
I don't want to miss a thing!
When we slow down, instead of hurrying to and fro,
and appreciate the wondrous beauty all around us,
we become the experience itself.
This is being in harmony with the Earth, herself.
And if you put your ear to the ground, you can hear her singing!
And this slow pace becomes almost effortless,
no matter what the terrain ahead brings.
I flow across the surface like a leaf in a stream,
And time ceases to worry me any longer.
All of a sudden,
I hardly notice the weight of the world on my back.

THE SCOOP ABOUT HAULING STUFF ON A WALK
If you are out for a short neighborhood walk, you may need absolutely nothing, or you may feel more comfortable having a few basic things with you. When l am out on a short neighborhood walk, l usually keep a bandana, headphones, pocketknife, cell phone, and a lemon-honey throat lozenge in my pocket. l drink a lot of water before l go so, l do not need to carry any if l am only gone for a short while. There is an indescribable sense of freedom in quickly putting on some appropriate shoes and heading out for a neighborhood walk.

If l am going on a hike in the woods, especially since l most likely will not have cell phone service, l carry a day pack or a large waist pack with additional items, such as 2+ liters of water, rain gear, a well-stocked first aid kit, snacks, etc. My personal guideline is always to be prepared to spend at least one night out in case of an unforeseen situation. It may not be the most comfortable night l have spent in the woods, but l would be safe and alive.

All recommended gear and clothing are listed in the next section, "*The Official WildWood Magic Day-Hiking Essentials & What to Wear List.*" If l am on a multi-day hiking trip, that is a much more comprehensive list. **(Check out my guide to *The 10 "Must-Haves" in Backpacking* gear on the www.WildWood-Magic.com website.)** The funny thing is, whether you call it walking, hiking, backpacking, or trekking, the only difference is the type of shoes you wear and the amount of "stuff" you need to haul!

BEING PREPARED
Walking in the woods can be the most awe-inspiring adventure ever. It can also be a total nightmare when attempted without proper planning, supplies, and preparation. Since safety and comfort are chief concerns, your knowledge, skills, and the

gear you choose to take with you into the backcountry are of great importance.

Getting into the backcountry safely and effectively takes solid skills and preparation. *Plan ahead and prepare*, the "Leave No Trace Center for Outdoor Ethic's" first principle, is the key to safe and fun outdoor adventures. Having the knowledge that you planned for the trip to the best of your ability allows you to have a more relaxed attitude and a serene experience in the outdoors. The mind isn't busy thinking up all the "what if's" because you have packed all necessary items to anticipate a wide variety of occurrences, and you (hopefully) have the skills and training to handle whatever comes your way.

With practice, trust in yourself, and a positive outlook, you will be a capable walker very quickly. To me, there is nothing that compares to it! The following lists include all the basics you will need to have on you and with you to be safe and thoroughly prepared for a walk in the woods. The lists are also very comprehensive on purpose. Remote backcountry hikes require more supplies than "front country" hikes or short walks close to home. Pack your gear according to the nature of the trek, duration, remoteness, intensity, weather, and the needs of your group.

THE OFFICIAL *WILDWOOD MAGIC* DAY-HIKING ESSENTIALS LIST:
- A Daypack or a Waistpack
- Adequate Food
- Adequate Water
- Compass/map/ hiking guide
- Cell phone
- Headlamp or flashlight
- Toilet paper
- First-aid and Gear Repair Kit
- Waterproof matches/lighter and Firestarter
- Extra clothes

- Pocketknife or multi-tool
- Hand sanitizer
- Bandana
- Emergency shelter
- Whistle
- Water filter/purifier or chemical treatment
- ID/Cash/Credit Card/Health Insurance card/Itinerary
- Walking stick or trekking poles
- Sunscreen/Sunglasses
- Trash bag or large Ziploc bag for trash

OTHER ITEMS TO CONSIDER:
- Insect Repellent
- Lip-Balm
- Journal And Pen/Pencil
- Binoculars
- Flora And Fauna Guide
- Trowel
- *Body Glide* Skin Lubricant (For Chafing)
- GPS
- Satellite Messenger Or A Personal Locator Beacon
- Altimeter Watch
- Gaiters (for rain, mud, debris, or snow)
- Trekking Umbrella (for sun and rain)
- Buff: I love Buffs! They are a versatile thin tube of fabric that can be used in various ways - around the neck, the ears, the hair, the whole head, as a face shield/mask, etc. They can also be pulled over a stuff sack and used as a handy "pillowcase" if needed.

DETAILED INFORMATION ABOUT THE GEAR IN THE LISTS

DAYPACKS
Daypacks have had many improvements in comfort and technology since the first days of school bookbags. Choose a day-

pack big enough to fit everything you need and is comfortable to wear for the length of your entire trip. Some daypacks have loops, straps, and pockets for just about any piece of gear imaginable.

Many outdoor sports have their own gear specific to the activity, such as climbing, mountaineering, ice climbing, trail running, or technical hiking. Check out your local outfitters and try on as many different styles as you can to find the right one that fits like a glove and holds everything you need for your kind of adventuring.

WAIST PACKS
Waist Packs (Also known as "Fanny Packs" or "Hip Pouches") come in a variety of shapes and sizes. They, too, have evolved over time, and some even have a built-in bladder system for hands-free hydration. I have had some that fit two-liter-sized water bottles on either side and a pouch in the middle, equivalent to a medium backpack! They also come small enough to hold only the contents of a slim wallet.

I have several that I use depending on the nature of the walk. Many people find it a more comfortable option because it eliminates strain on the back and shoulders by focusing the weight around the hips and waist. Be sure to keep the weight evenly distributed on your body. Choosing one with a broader hip belt can also make it more comfortable to wear.

FOOD
Proper nutrition is a crucial element for optimal health and energy. Different body types require different amounts and types of food. While doing your research and experimentation, choose foods for sustained nutrition, such as high protein, dense foods like nuts and seeds, as well as high carb, quick-energy foods such as fruit, sweets, and grains. Just like trying on different footwear, exploring the best breakfast foods before your morning walk, or the best trail snacks for your level of ac-

tivity, is a matter of personal taste, individual needs, and willingness to experiment.

When packing food for a hike, choose nonperishable items, especially on very hot days. And if you do carry perishable items, eat them early on your walk. It doesn't take long for some foods to spoil or oils to become rancid. If you bring snacks prone to getting crushed, like a sandwich or crackers, packing them in a rigid, plastic food container is a good option, although it does add some weight.

Be mindful of how you place food in your pack to keep it in its original shape. Pack your snacks on the top of your backpack or in the middle to help insulate them from extreme temperatures. Of course, after a long, arduous hike, any food -squished or not- tastes pretty good, right? And Always bring more food than you think you need. You never know when that extra fuel might be required by you or someone in your group.

WHAT TO PACK TO EAT: CALORIES VS. NUTRITION
Before you pack a daypack full of candy bars and sugary treats, please allow me to share a personal learning experience. When I first started hiking regularly, I chose to eat mostly comfort foods ...you know... as a reward for all the energy that I expended on my day's adventure. I earned it, right??? Whenever I got to my destination, I would whip out my candy-filled trail mixes, sugary cookies, and candy bars to munch. I had no idea I was actually depleting my energy by consuming only highly caloric, "quick energy" snacks.

I also ate this way the entire time I was on my six-month trek on the Appalachian Trail. The general thinking at the time was calories in, calories out. Everyone I spoke to about food seemed only to be concerned with the number of calories they were consuming. No, no, and no! Those foods have almost zero nutritional value. Even energy bars labeled as "all-natural" or "healthy" (or whatever marketing hooey they are allowed to print on the pack-aging) are usually junk food, with a few exceptions, of course.

The more processed the food is, the less whole nutrition it has in it. When choosing foods for whole health, think of natural foods as much as possible. Today, my go-to snacks for walks and hikes are generally fruits, veggies, nuts, and seeds. Yes, these foods are heavier to carry, but it is worth it to have en-durance, stamina, and sustained energy. I often think about how much more energy I would have had and how much better I would have felt if I had been eating more nutritious foods along the way.

The more whole, unprocessed foods, veggies, and fruits you have in your diet, the better you will feel. I believe every "body" has different dietary needs, but this is a fundamental principle of eat-ing to feel energized and nourished. The foods we choose to eat *most of the time* are such an essential part of our body's ability to heal, handle stressful situations, and perform all the tasks at hand. By taking responsibility for our health by fueling the body with proper nutrition, ensures we are rewarded with strength and endurance in all of our endeavors.

Like almost everything in life, finding what works for you is a process of experimentation. Moderation still rules the roost. And there is plenty of room to get creative with healthy food options. There are excellent resources and recipe books available for people on the go, for every kind of diet.

WATER
Water is as important as nutritious food. Hydrating yourself continuously, during and before any kind of exercise, is ex-tremely important. Dehydration is almost always avoidable and a much bigger problem than many realize. The side effects list is long and can be counterintuitive for figuring out what is hap-pening. Frequently drinking water on a hike will allow your

body to flush out toxins, keep your body's cells adequately hydrated, and keep your energy level high.

The amount you need depends on several factors such as the length of the hike and the conditions. My general guideline is that when I go for a moderate walk over 5 miles, I bring at least 2 liters of water (or more). If it is a very long hike or especially difficult, I carry some type of additional water treatment with me, especially when it's sweltering out, and I might be sweating more. For my morning walks or short hikes, I will take less and make sure I am well hydrated before leaving. Always bring more than you think you will need.

WATER CONTAINERS

There are several ways to carry water. Standard plastic reusable bottles, such as the brand *Nalgene*, are ubiquitous. You rarely see people using the old-style canteens that once were so popular but are sometimes still available in military surplus and sporting-goods stores. Metal insulated bottles are great for keeping cold or hot liquids but can be quite heavy to carry. However, I have been known to take an insulated bottle full of hot tea on a cold day-hike, a time or two!

Another option is a *bladder hydration system*, which is a leakproof bag that fits into a sleeve in your backpack with a tube coming out, equipped with a mouthpiece at the end. Today's technology has made this a great option to have 1, 2, or even 3 liters of water readily available. However, you must stay aware of how much you are consuming so you don't run out too quickly.

Bladders are especially awesome when you have water filtration or treatment options with you to refill the bladder when you need it. Because they are bags, they form-fit into the space you place them in, so they can take up much less room than traditional bottles. When purchasing a daypack, be sure to choose

one with the necessary "hydration system compatible" compo-
nents, mainly the sleeve and an opening for the tube to come out,
if you want to use this type of water container.

Although plenty of people do it, it is not recommended to add
"water flavor enhancements" to hydration bladders because
any leftover residue may mold or mildew if not regularly and
thoroughly cleaned. There are usually brand-specific cleaning
kits available, but the corners of the bladder and the tubes are
challenging to clean. However, it is so tempting because many
of the bladders cause the water to taste like plastic. Ewwww.

COMPASS/MAP/HIKING GUIDE FOR THE AREA
Being familiar with where you are hiking is essential. Having a
map is always prudent, and the skills to use a compass will give
you more faith to explore with confidence. In remote backcountry areas, I like having a good guidebook for the place I am
adventuring. You can also make photocopies of the pages you
know you will be navigating if you do not want to carry the
weight of the entire book.

You can always use a phone GPS trail app or "screenshots" of a
trail map or book pages, but I recommend having an actual
map. After all, maps don't break or have batteries that can run
down. However, they can get wet. Keep any paper maps or
trail guide pages in a resealable plastic bag. Some maps are
printed on waterproof paper, such as the *National Geographic
Trails Illustrated Maps.* Water-resistant maps are typically labeled as such.

CELL PHONE
Phone or no phone? Although I am a dedicated advocate for getting away from technology and just BEing in nature, I always carry
my cell phone with me for several reasons. They can [sometimes]
be useful to have in emergencies. Always assume cell service is

unreliable or unavailable in the backcountry, so never depend on having service as your emergency back-up plan.

It is also safer to carry a phone with you if you need a flashlight or to use the countless helpful apps available to track steps and your route. Make sure your phone is fully charged before you leave and close down all battery-sucking apps. I try to reduce my phone battery consumption while in the woods by keeping the phone on airplane mode, dimming the screen brightness, and turning off battery-killers like Wifi and Bluetooth.

If I am on a proper nature hike, I keep my phone on airplane mode because I choose to experience my walks as moving meditations. I do not want to hear notifications, texts, or other human-made noises. However, I love taking photographs, which is why I don't turn it completely off. If I am on an urban walk, I might wear headphones and listen to a podcast or an audiobook. All that being said, I believe it is essential to spend time in nature without the interference of devices, at least some of the time. Your relationship with technology is something you can consciously decide for yourself based on your needs and desires.

HEADLAMP OR FLASHLIGHT

Headlamps are one of the most convenient modern-day inventions! Look, Ma, no hands! Having a hands-free beam of light pointing toward where you are looking is solid genius! It also opens the potential for some exciting night hikes for the extra-adventurous. Today, many styles use super-bright LED bulbs that last a long time and don't use up batteries too quickly. They have adjustable stretchy headbands that are comfortable and fit just about anybody. Make sure the batteries are new or fully charged. Consider bringing a set of spare batteries on longer trips. For longer battery life, take the batteries out to store headlamps and flashlights for long periods.

TOILET PAPER

I'm pretty sure I don't need to explain why this is important to have, but here goes anyway. Always bring adequate supplies for bathroom breaks for everyone in your group. Although listed in the list for "Other items to consider," packing a lightweight trowel in addition to toilet paper in your daypack will ensure that waste can be properly disposed of while hiking. I keep biodegradable toilet paper (for #2 only), hand sanitizer, and an ultralight trowel in a small stuff sack that I take with me anytime I go for a hike in the woods. **(Please see the "Leave No Trace" section about disposing of waste properly.)**

FIRST AID AND GEAR REPAIR KIT
(See First-Aid chapter for a complete list.)
A properly stocked first-aid kit includes remedies for an assortment of issues. Also, bring any regular and emergency medication you might need, such as an EpiPen or rescue inhaler if you have a history of allergic reactions or breathing issues. Ensure you have ample supplies for treating blisters, the most common yet potentially serious problem you will most likely need to remedy.

It is a good idea to have a few emergency gear repair items on longer hikes, such as duct tape/Gorilla tape, paracord, extra zip bags, garbage bags, and zip ties. You know, in case you want to get all MacGyver on the trail and impress your friends by fixing their stuff.

WATERPROOF MATCHES/LIGHTER AND FIRE STARTER
Making a fire in the backcountry may be necessary for emergency signaling or extra warmth. Keeping the body warm and dry is extremely important to prevent and treat hypothermia. Hypothermia can occur even in warm conditions. Plus, campfires are cool! Starting big fires is not. Be careful with fire and never leave a fire unattended or smoldering. **(Please, please,**

please see the "Leave No Trace" section about Minimizing Campfire Impacts.)

Bring waterproof, windproof matches, usually found in a sporting goods department. They still need to be appropriately stored in a watertight container because even waterproof matches can get soggy. However, waterproof matches can often be more reliable than lighters, especially low-quality ones.

EXTRA CLOTHES

It is essential to have an extra layer or two of clothing- more than you think you need- especially in terrain where the weather can radically change from one moment to the next. **(See the next section for a full list of essential clothing and the advantages/disadvantages of various technical fabrics.)**

POCKETKNIFE OR MULTITOOL

Multi-tools come in a wide variety of styles with any option you can think of, including a corkscrew. I personally refuse to carry a multi-tool with a corkscrew, but I digress. I carry a sheathed knife and a small pair of medical scissors that I keep in my first aid kit. Choose your tools based on personal needs and the safety know-how to use them properly. Store all tools in a place where they are not likely to get damp but handy enough to have them when you need them. What does MacGyver carry in his pocket??

HAND SANITIZER

Hand sanitizer comes in convenient, small refillable sizes perfect for a daypack or a fanny pack. Be aware that some varieties are scented and will need to be stored appropriately with other "smellables" on overnight hikes. Cooties are everywhere. Keep your hands clean. :-)

BANDANA

Bandanas are great to have as a "boogie-rag," something to wipe the sweat off your brow, a washcloth, an emergency water pre-filter, a neckerchief... you name it! There are endless uses for this basic but fundamental piece of gear. Some even have useful information such as plant identification, a trail maps, or other cool stuff!

EMERGENCY SHELTER

In a backcountry setting, an emergency shelter could be a life-saving addition to your daypack. Being able to devise makeshift protection from the elements can be the difference between life and death due to exposure, frostbite, hypothermia, etc. An emergency shelter can be a couple of trash bags, some duct tape, and paracord. Several brands manufacture pre-packaged emergency shelters and bivy sacks. (Bivy is short for bivouac sack.)

WHISTLE

It is a good idea to attach a whistle to your backpack to have in an emergency. Remember, a customary call for help is three short blasts. Many packs have whistles built into the buckle of the sternum strap, which is the adjustable strap connecting the two shoulder straps going across the chest. Although these are typically not the loudest, these buckle whistles are handy by their proximity to the mouth and ease of use.

WATER FILTER/PURIFIER OR CHEMICAL TREATMENT

Generating potable water, especially in very hot weather or emergencies, can be the difference between life and death. There are numerous ways to purify water; however, many of these involve bulky equipment better suited to multi-day hikes. A lightweight, portable option is to store water treatment tablets in your emergency kit. You can always build a fire and boil water, but this requires a pot to boil the water! If you are already carrying the kitchen sink, you may as well have a light-weight water filter!

ID/CASH/CREDIT CARD/HEALTH INSURANCE CARD/ITINERARY

Having cash on hand is helpful because some trails require permits and fees. It is also vital that you have identification on you at all times. It a good idea to keep any pertinent medical information such as blood type or allergies, emergency contacts, and any insurance information with you. Be sure to give a local person your itinerary details and inform them when you expect to return.

WALKING STICK OR TREKKING POLES

Many people find this optional, or ...gasp... even silly, but I do not. A walking stick or trekking poles are invaluable for assisting with balance, personal safety, and having confidence while crossing streams. When used correctly, a pair of poles take many pounds of pressure off your knees and transform your walk into a full-body workout. I typically bring trekking poles when I hike with a heavier pack and a walking stick anytime I walk or day-hike off-pavement.

If you are not used to having a stick or poles in your hands, when you first begin they can feel a little awkward. However, it doesn't take too much time to feel as though they are an extension of your arms. The advantages are significant, particularly if you have feet, knee, or hip problems or any concerns with balance. Eventually, you will wonder how you ever hiked without them!

SUNSCREEN/SUNGLASSES

Sun protection (including a brimmed hat and long-sleeves) is vital, especially in areas where you are exposed to harsh UV rays for extended periods, such as above the tree-line and areas with limited or no shade. In buggy times, sunglasses can help keep the little buggers out of your eyes. Plus, your friends won't be able to tell when you're rolling your eyes at them!

TRASH BAG (OR A LARGE ZIPLOC BAG) FOR TRASH

Bring a designated bag (or two) to haul out trash and any litter you find with you. Packing out a sticky apple core is a lot less messy with a little forethought. Part of *Walking as a Sacred Path* is taking responsibility for the lands we walk upon as if they are our own. Leaving our picnic spots nicer than we find them is respecting the Earth and makes you feel fantastic! I double-dog dare you to try it.

> *"...the care of the earth is our most ancient and most worthy and, after all, our most pleasing responsibility. To cherish what remains of it, and to foster its renewal, is our only legitimate hope."*
> —Wendell Berry

WHAT SHOULD I WEAR?

ESSENTIAL CLOTHING: THINK IN LAYERS
- Well-fitting, comfortable trail shoes or hiking boots
- Good quality wool/synthetic socks
- Base layer/breathable short-sleeved shirt
- Long-sleeved wicking shirt and/or a long-sleeved thin fleece
- Quick-drying pants/shorts/skirts/skorts
- Waterproof/breathable rain jacket and pants
- Sunhat/Warm hat and Gloves
- Insulated layer/Jacket
- Long underwear

HIKING SHOES OR BOOTS

Choose footwear that is well-fitting and comfortable right from the start. Walk in them until they feel well broken-in before venturing too far from home. Shoe selection is a process of research and experimentation with brands and styles that suit all the particulars of your feet. Shop at quality local outfitters to get professional help from fellow outdoor enthusiasts. **(See the FEET section for detailed information about shoes and feet.)**

GOOD QUALITY SOCKS

The number one rule is NO cotton socks. Cotton will get wet, stay wet, and cause hot spots and blisters. Choose wool or synthetic materials. Merino wool is considered to be the best, but some people prefer wicking synthetic blends.

BASELAYER/BREATHABLE SHORT-SLEEVED SHIRT

On any given hike, you may experience times of intense heat as well as cooler, wet weather. Ideally, your base layer should be thin enough to keep you as cool as possible in warm weather while still giving you ample coverage for sun or wind. If you are wearing a backpack, tank tops can cause painful chafing under the backpack straps, especially along the collarbones. A quick-dry, short-sleeved shirt is a better option for layering.

LONG-SLEEVED WICKING SHIRT, OR A LONG-SLEEVED THIN FLEECE

In cooler weather, wear several thin layers that can be added or removed as needed. Wearing several thin layers will trap air and body heat between the layers and keep you warmer than just having one thick layer. You will also be able to regulate your temperature much better by having more options. Thin layers will also dry faster when they are wet.

Always have a long-sleeved layer with you, even in warmer months. The weather, especially at higher altitudes, can change suddenly, any time of the year. Even on the hottest day, rainstorms can arrive suddenly and soak you to the point where you can get chilled. Hypothermia can happen in warm seasons as well as cold ones. It is always a good idea to have additional warm, dry layers. You will be happy you have them!

QUICK-DRYING PANTS & SHORTS

First of all, jeans, no matter how great they look on you, should be nowhere, I mean absolutely nowhere, in your hiking-clothing repertoire. Lightweight, quick-dry pants are the best option, especially if you are unsure what the terrain is like, even in summer.

Pants are great if there is any chance a trail is overgrown, which is quite common in the summer. Long pants are also handy for keeping ticks and other bitey things off of you, sun protection, as well as avoiding a brush by poison ivy, poison oak, or other rash-producing vegetation. Convertible pants are a super convenient option, as you will have a pair of pants and shorts, all in one. Cool, huh? The legs "zip-off" and turn them into shorts.

SKIRTS & SKORTS

I also like to wear hiking skirts made of quick-dry nylon. If I know a trail is clear of overgrown brush and poison ivy, I wear a skirt in warm months because I find them much cooler to wear. Skirts are easier to take a pit stop with, and the swooshing action of the hem actually keeps bugs off my legs. (And, I sew them myself, so I am freakishly fashionable.) Skorts are popular for walking as well and are essentially skirts with a pair of shorts built-in underneath. Skorts... They're not just for golfers!

WATERPROOF/BREATHABLE RAIN JACKET AND PANTS

Do yourself a huge favor and invest in a set of high quality, breathable, waterproof rain gear made from Gore-Tex® or some other wildly expensive... I mean effective... material that will shed water during sudden downpours. It is crucial to stay dry and warm in inclement weather. Leave that supercheap PU (polyurethane) rain getup at home.

Although it has a more tempting price tag, you may as well wrap yourself in garbage bags because it is the same effect. You could overheat and be as wet from sweating as you would be in the pouring rain, although with some added dehydration. And it's usually pretty heavy stuff.

PONCHOS & OTHER RAIN ACCESSORIES

Some people prefer a rain poncho in hot weather. They are available in different lengths, and some have extra room to cover your backpack, too. You can also find other cool rain gear items such as "rain wraps," which is basically a waterproof wrap skirt and rain mittens to go over your hands while using trekking poles. Wahoo! Stay dry and be stylish all at the same time!

SUNHAT/WARM HAT AND GLOVES

A lightweight, brimmed hat is appropriate for every season of the year to keep sun or rain off your face. It is also a good idea to always have a warm beanie-styled hat and gloves in chilly temperatures or hiking in areas where the weather can change rapidly. I carry a pair of thin glove liners year-round while I am day-hiking and backpacking, and I am so often happy I have them. Choose whatever style is appropriate for the terrain, your hike, and potential weather.

INSULATED LAYER/JACKET

In warmer weather, you may only need a rain jacket and an extra layer or two. In cooler weather or high-altitude treks, you may need an insulated jacket. These are available in a variety of options depending on the features you need. I cannot stress enough how important it is to stay warm and dry in all outdoor conditions. Choose an insulating layer that is appropriate for the terrain, your hike, and potential weather.

LONG UNDERWEAR/THERMALS/BASE LAYERS

In cold conditions, extra layers are essential in keeping the body warm. Choose wool, silk, or synthetic materials for undergarments. As part of my extra clothing on overnight hikes, I keep a set of thin silk or wool long underwear. I have been happy to have them on many occasions. Thermals are usually available in three options: lightweight, midweight, or heavyweight.

"I only went out for a walk and finally concluded to stay out till sundown, for going out, I found, was really going in."
—John Muir

CHOOSING THE RIGHT FABRIC

FABRICS... SYNTHETICS, SILK, AND WOOL
When selecting suitable base layers for outdoor activities, choose synthetic, silk, wool, or a wool blend fabric so it will dry quickly and prevent chafing. Always avoid cotton, as it takes a very long time to dry and can seriously rub wet skin and make you cold when it inevitably gets wet. Wool is naturally antimicrobial and antibacterial. It resists molds, mildew, and bacteria, so you can wear it much longer before you smell like a skunk.

Silk will absorb slightly more moisture and takes a while longer to dry than synthetic materials. Silk is also highly breathable; therefore, it is not as warm as wool. Silks are commonly used in base layers but are generally considered lightweight and traditionally worn in warmer climates.

Synthetics are usually more durable than other materials but absorb and retain odor-causing bacteria more than natural fibers. Of course, smelling like a skunk is totally acceptable when you're hiking your tail off, so wear it like a badge of honor. You might as well because once they get stinky, it's hard to get them smelling like a rose again, but you can try.

One method to remove the odor is to soak your synthetic material clothing in bicarbonate (baking soda) before washing. I have had success adding a small amount of white vinegar to the mix.

Also, never use fabric softener on moisture-wicking clothing as it will clog the hollow, moisture-wicking fibers and will no longer be breathable.

FABRICS... NYLON, POLYESTER, & STRETCHY STUFF
Most hiking pants and shorts are made of nylon, polyester, or a blend. Nylon is softer than polyester; however, they both wick moisture away from the body and dry quickly. Walking and hiking pants commonly now have a small amount of stretchy material added, such as spandex, lycra, or elastane, for a wider range of mobility and comfort. And who doesn't love them some stretchy pants!!

> *"Walking is the perfect way of moving if you want to
> see into the life of things. It is the one way of freedom.
> If you go to a place on anything but your own feet,
> you are taken there too fast and miss a thousand delicate
> joys that were waiting for you by the wayside."*
> —Elizabeth von Arnim

Chapter 8
I KNOW YOU ARE EXCITED ABOUT A SECTION CALLED FEET!

Walk with your head held high!
Fling your wild nature up into the clouds!
Keep your two feet firmly on the ground...
And allow them to lead you to all things good,
All things that compel you
toward the next right step.
...For the breadcrumbs of spirit
Lead us on a remarkable journey
If we can just get out of the way!
Why walk?
Because going any faster
Could slow you down.

APPRECIATE THE FEET!

I would like to begin this fun and exciting section about all-things-feet by encouraging you to send some love and appreci-ation to this part of your body. They carry us around, all day, every day, and deserve recognition for their loyal and dedicated service. Although feet are generally some of the most under-valued parts of the body, the feet contain 52, or one-quarter, of all the bones in the human body. Many of us never appreciate our feet until we have problems with them. Then, we become uncomfortably aware of how convenient it is to move around freely at will.

Feet are not one of our more visually appreciated appendages; therefore, feet issues can often go totally ignored until they make their presence be sorely known. They can make life a breeze, and feet can make life miserable. Absolutely. Wretch-edly. Miserable. Walk for a few days in heavy rain with several blisters in wet boots to see the power that our little itsy-bitsy feet have over us!

Nurturing my feet has become one of my most important self-care rituals. As a walker, hiker, and long-distance backpacker, I am well aware that my load-bearing feet are the most central parts of my body. Fortunately, we can avoid many painful feet conditions simply by being mindful and learning a little self-care.

Taking care of your feet might initiate a new appreciation for your whole body. By sending love and gratitude to your feet, particularly if you are having any sort of difficulties, you begin fostering a positive, evidence-based healing relationship with your whole physical body. Feet tell us what they need to feel supported, which in turn develops inner trust.

It could be that you spend too much time on your feet, and they are merely calling for you to rest. Or, they could be calling for more action, asking you to stretch and take more walks. Give your feet whatever love and attention they need. Walk gently and often. Make friends with someone who likes to rub feet. :-) These are just a few ways to give the feet a little well-deserved appreciation. Love your feet! They can take you anywhere you wish to go!

SHOE-OFF BREAKS and OTHER EASY MIRACLE REMEDIES

One of my best walking tips ever, I figured out after spending three days off-trail trying to heal several severe blisters while hiking the Appalachian Trail. I had many problems with my feet at the beginning of my 2,200-mile journey. Literally, from about mile 20 to the minute I stepped up on the signboard at the summit of Katahdin, I had foot problems, off and on, nearly the entire way. I learned many helpful things, but my biggest takeaways were the importance of "shoe-off" breaks, foot powder, and the benefits of wearing the right sock liners and shoe inserts.

Thankfully when I walk now, I don't have as many issues as I did on that long walk. I would not have had nearly the troubles had I known then what I know now. Every single foot is different, and many remedies can help any shoe or boot perform and feel better. Not that all boots and shoes are good! If you want to be a proficient walker and hiker, you will have to experiment with different brands and combinations.

Let's start with the basics, like taking breaks during long walks. This easy fix is as simple as it sounds but way more necessary than you may think. Take regular breaks after every 2 - 3 hours of walking and remove your shoes and socks to let your feet rest, check them for potential problems, and let them completely dry out.

It is vital to the health of your feet to physically let them air and dry out, especially if they have been wet for a while. If you have planned extra time, shoe-off breaks are an excellent opportunity to cool your tootsies off in a creek or sit with your feet on the earth. Allow your feet enough time to dry off completely. You may even want to find a spot of sunshine to dry out your socks on a warm rock. I cannot stress how beneficial this little exercise is for your feet!

These breaks also give you a chance to check for hot spots or chaffing that you may not have noticed while walking. It is imperative to catch forming blisters as soon as possible. If you feel any pain or discomfort, always stop and examine your feet immediately. Blisters can quickly become infected, cause a great deal of pain, and can become serious problems. **(See the First Aid chapter for detailed information about treating blisters.)**

FIND A GREAT MEDITATION SPOT
Another excellent reason for a shoe-off-break is to slow down and enjoy the scenery. Dipping my feet in a cold creek on a warm summer day is one of my most treasured activities when I am on a hike in the woods. Places where I hike frequently usually have a location that draws me to it, and I find myself taking my shoes off and meditating on the earth without even thinking about it.

Even while walking and hiking for fun, many of us fall prey to the allure of the destination-focused mindset. Taking our time to enjoy the scenery, be present, and soak in all the healing qualities of nature can significantly enhance our experience. By incorporating shoe-off-breaks into your day's itinerary, you will not only enjoy the benefits of healthy, happy feet, but a light heart as well.

MANY PAINS IN THE BODY ORIGINATE FROM THE FEET!
Even being a daily walker and hiker for decades, I still get annoying little aches and pains. I have a go-to remedy for most minor feet, joint, and knee pains... you know... the minor "tweak" that just pops up out of nowhere? This solution is kind of like the quick fix for most computer problems, where you turn it off and unplug everything for a minute and then turn it back on again? My remedy is just as simple, and it is tightening up both of the laces on both shoes.

When I feel a little discomfort in a foot, a knee, or even a sudden back pain, usually retying my shoes really helps! Sometimes it needs a total reboot, pun intended, by taking both shoes and socks completely off (and enjoying some shoe-off time for a few minutes) and then putting everything back on again and lacing up both shoes a little tighter. I know, it sounds ridiculous and too good to be true, but it works!

It is also important to retie *both* shoes, as they both may have loosened up while walking, but also because where we feel the pain may not be the leg, foot, or knee that needs the extra support. Making micro-adjustments to the way your shoes fit can alleviate pain, discomfort, and numbness. It is important not to tie your shoes overly tightly, just snug enough to feel well-supported.

OTHER QUICK FIXES: SHOE LACING OPTIONS
When you are experiencing chronic foot pain, it is hard to concentrate on anything else. The good news is that several different lacing options can help solve the most common issues. There can be an immediate, noticeable improvement when you implement the correct technique to solve the source of discomfort. The following common lacing techniques can completely change how a shoe or boot fits.

THE CONCERN: WIDE FEET
THE BENEFIT: This lacing technique can help loosen the entire shoe, giving the feet more overall space.
THE TECHNIQUE: Begin by threading the shoelace in a criss-cross pattern and skip every other eyelet.

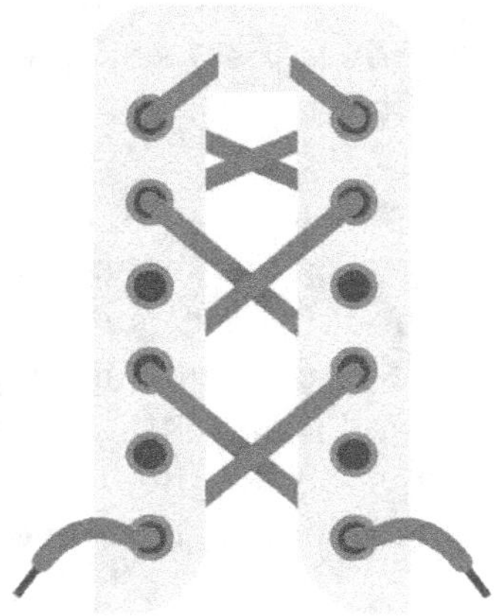

THE CONCERN: NARROW FEET
THE BENEFIT: This lacing technique can significantly tighten the entire shoe, giving a more secure feel and added support.
THE TECHNIQUE: Thread the shoelace in a crisscross pattern and skip an eyelet in the center.

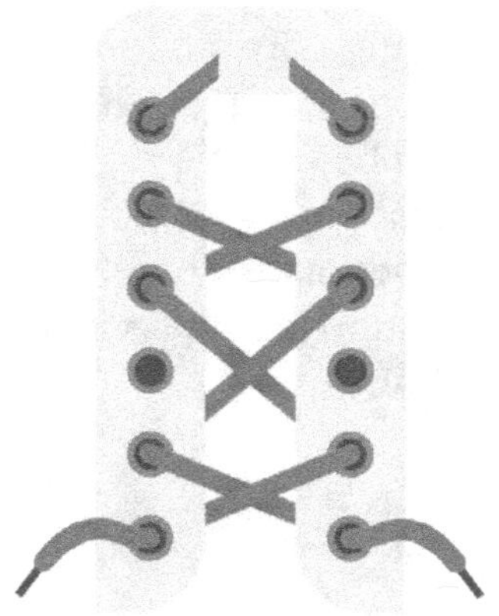

THE CONCERN: HEEL SLIPPAGE
THE BENEFIT: This method supports the ankle and will secure the heel without making the whole shoe feel too tight.
THE TECHNIQUE: Lace the shoes in the regular pattern until the second-to-last eyelet, then lace straight up into the last hole without crisscrossing the laces, and then thread the shoelace through the loop on the other side, and then tie the laces securely.

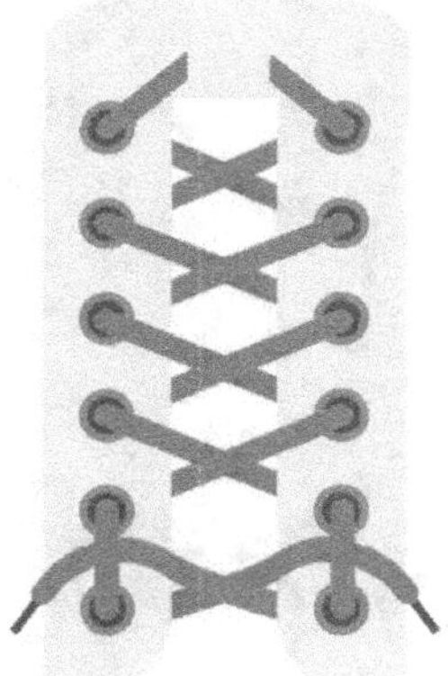

THE CONCERN: SHOES ARE GENERALLY JUST TOO DANG TIGHT!
THE BENEFIT: This lacing option will help take the pressure off the entire foot by evenly spacing the shoelaces.
THE TECHNIQUE: Lace the shoelaces by threading one underneath every other eyelet, parallel on the top with no crisscrossing.

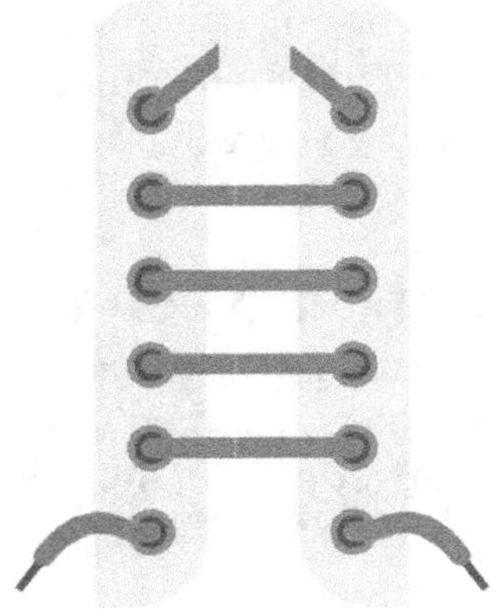

THE CONCERN: WIDE FOREFOOT
THE BENEFIT: This lacing technique effectively creates extra room in the forefoot while creating more support toward the ankle.
THE TECHNIQUE: "Window Box Lacing" Lace the shoelaces up the sides of the first two eyelets, eliminating the crisscross until the middle of the foot, then begin the standard crisscrossing pattern and tie securely as usual.

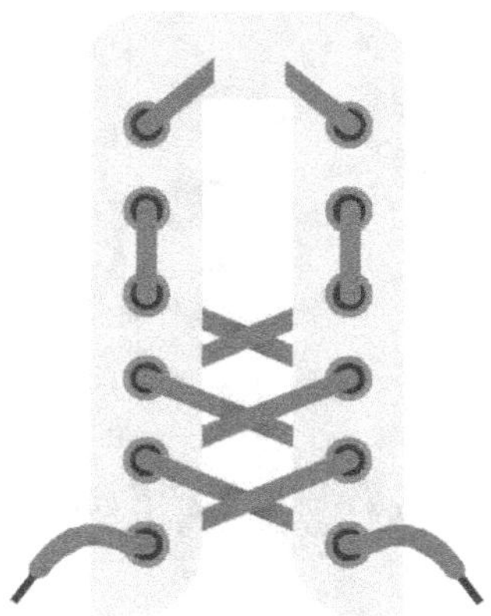

FOOTCARE FOR WALKERS
It isn't just the fundamental quality and fit of our footwear and socks that matters; basic foot care is critical as well. The feet are the most vital body parts when it comes to walking. For our feet to perform their absolute best, we need to take good care of them. Doing anything besides clipping the toenails might be a new concept for some, but when you become addicted to the magic of walking, as I know you will, foot care will become second nature.

PUMICE-STONES, FOOT CREAM & FOOT POWDER
The first step is keeping the feet clean, smooth, dry, and fungus-free. Keep your toenails trimmed to the shortest comfortable level. If you tend to get painful ingrown toenails, don't clip the corners, just cut them straight across after you get out of

the shower when they tend to be a little softer. If the corners
are dagger-like, use a fine nail file to gently soften the corners
without rounding them too much.

I also like to use a natural *pumice stone* on my feet where I
usually get thick callouses, such as the outside of my heels. A
word of caution here; it is entirely possible to over-use a
pumice stone or other feet-scouring implement. Being in tune
with our body sounds obvious enough, but many of our self-
care rituals are performed without much thought. Self-care is a
nurturing practice of becoming aware of the needs of our body.
It is beneficial to be particularly mindful while scrubbing extra
skin off the bottoms of our feet. Go easy, my friend!

Another helpful footcare tool is a good *heel balm,* such as my
favorite, Flexitol, that can help smooth rough, dry, cracked skin.
I slather on this foot exfoliant and moisturizer after I bathe and
then put on clean socks to let it soak in well. Natural oils such
as coconut oil are also great to use on the feet, although it can
make them slippery, so please be careful. I also like to use *foot
powder*, such as Gold Bond, on my feet at night, especially on
multi-day hikes. Heel balm and foot powder are big parts of my
happy feet ritual.

Primary foot care could be just adding a step or two in our daily
hygiene rituals, and the feet are all the happier for these simple
things. If we take care of them, they will take care of us. It isn't
just a silly statement; it's how these things work. The human
body is absolutely miraculous. Our body is continually healing
and repairing itself from what we do to it with food, water, air,
and scrubby things!

GET A PEDICURE!
If you are not the best at taking care of your feet, I suggest
finding a reputable establishment for a relaxing, healthy pedicure. Oh, how my feet do love a good pedicure! Like every-

thing, there are clean, high-quality nail salons, and then there are others. If you don't know of one, get recommendations from friends you know and trust. I like to treat myself to a pedicure before I go out on a long hike.

DRY FEET ARE HAPPY FEET!

We have established that taking care of the feet is a top priority. Sometimes the biggest challenge is just keeping them dry. It is relatively straightforward to keep the body dry, with all the various options available today ...rain jackets, rain pants, ponchos, rain hats, and even lightweight trekking umbrellas.

Keeping the feet dry and comfortable, on the other hand, can be more challenging. Conditions such as trench foot, athletes' foot, repetitive friction, and other issues can be triggered by walking with wet feet for extended periods. These can create a dangerous condition if left untreated.

There are two opposing schools of thought about footwear for wet conditions. Waterproof shoes and boots, such as those made with Gore-Tex® or other waterproof, breathable fabrics, are standard solutions, along with accessories such as gaiters. Wearing gaiters can keep water and debris from entering the top of your shoes/boots. They come in all kinds of shapes, sizes, and materials but basically cover the tops of your boots and hook over your laces and/or around the bottom of the shoe. The downside is they can be bulky and hot and are just something else you have to carry when you inevitably take them off.

The other perspective is to wear lightweight, fast-drying shoes or even hiking sandals. This option will provide less support and will get saturated very quickly but will dry much faster. These types of shoes, similar to trail running shoes, can initially feel good on your feet but may have long term consequences if you carry a heavy backpack, have a tendency to roll your ankles, or have knee or hip issues. Personally, I find that no matter where I am walking, on a trail, or in the city walking on pavement, my feet and ankles prefer more support. Once again, this is a personal experiment in finding what works for you.

TIPS FOR WET SHOES & FEET:

- Remove the insoles from your shoes and loosen the laces as much as possible to help them dry out.

- If you are out on a hike, change your socks regularly. Bring extra pairs of moisture-wicking socks. Wring out wet socks and hang them from your backpack or keep them close to your body so your body heat will speed up the drying process.

- Dry out your shoes by stuffing them with absorbent materials such as newspaper. However, do not leave wet materials packed in there too long, or they will begin to mildew. Mold for sure won't help your sweaty walking shoes smell better. Ask me how I know.

- Friction and chaffing can be much worse when your feet and shoes are wet, not to mention a veritable fungus playground. An anti-chafing skin lubricant can prevent hotspots and blisters from forming. These types of products usually come in stick form, gel, or "liquid powder" form.

- Most importantly, listen to your feet. Treat any pain, discomfort, or hot spots immediately. Do not keep going until it's more convenient. Time is of the essence! Thoroughly dry and clean your feet at the first sensation of pain, numbness, or itching.

*"I firmly believe that with the right footwear,
one can rule the world."*
—Bette Midler

HOW TO CHOOSE THE RIGHT PAIR OF SHOES OR BOOTS

FOOTWEAR: WHERE DO I START?
Having the proper gear is essential for any activity, especially an adventure that can sometimes take us far away from home. Thankfully, there isn't much you really need. The most important purchase you will make concerning the activity of walking is anything going on your feet. Seek professional help. Randomly buying stuff on the internet is okay for some things, but a long shot for finding high quality, well-fitting footwear, unless you already know the brand or particular shoe works for you.

Footwear is not the place to skimp. Since it is the only piece of "gear" you actually need, other than good quality socks, you will benefit from investing in the health and happiness of your feet.

Most shoes will loosen up slightly after wearing and breaking them in. However, never buy shoes that feel too big or too tight, right out of the box. Unfortunately, we never really know exactly how the shoes or boots ultimately fit until we have worn them a time or two or three on a walk.

Also, most feet fluctuate in size slightly depending on how much you walk, weather conditions, and hormonal fluctuations in the human body. All of these considerations can make shoe-buying extremely challenging. However, do not get discouraged. It is easier than ever to do research online first, ask other walkers and hikers, and try out different styles that appeal to you.

HOW TO BUY FOOTWEAR FOR WALKING & HIKING

For pavement walking, find a good running shoe store that has knowledgeable employees and a good reputation. They will often watch you walk around the store to evaluate which pair of shoes looks right on your feet. Some even utilize these amazing high-tech devices that you stand on as the machine measures your foot from every angle! Shoe buying has undoubtedly changed over the years.

The same goes for trail shoes or hiking boots. Find a local outfitter to help you get fitted for the shoe appropriate for the adventures you are planning. They usually know all the benefits and problems of all the brands they carry and what foot type works well with which shoes. With all the options out there, it makes all the difference finding reliable help.

NO PAIN, NO GAIN DOES NOT APPLY HERE!

When comparing options, try walking around the store and going up and down an incline or stairs. Evaluate how much movement there is inside the shoes and whether or not there are any uncomfortable sensations. In any walking footwear, you should be able to wiggle your toes easily and have a thumb's distance between the end of your toes and the end of the shoe.

Shoes should fit snugly but never tightly. You should not feel any seams or stitching, and the shoes should feel generally comfortable. The best time to try on shoes is late afternoon or the evening, particularly after walking around during the day when your feet are the largest size.

Choose quality shoes with the right support for your type of feet, a stable heel with a flexible outsole, and adequate shock absorption in the midsole. If you already wear inserts or orthotics, bring them with you to try on shoes. Also, try on your boots or shoes with the same socks you plan to wear with them. Since socks vary significantly in thickness and cushioning, it can dramatically change the way shoes or boots fit.

Often shoe retailers will let you try shoes and return them if they are not right for you. Try walking around indoors with the shoes before taking them on a walk outdoors. I always recommend finding a small, independently operated outfitter, as they will be the most knowledgeable about current shoes and styles, as well as the most passionate and enthusiastic! After all, they are also usually the ones out there wearing them, too.

> *"One shoe can change your life."*
> —Cinderella

TYPES OF WALKING, HIKING, & BACKPACKING FOOTWEAR & CLASSIC USAGE:

- *Running or walking shoes* are the least supportive, have little to no break-in period, and are the best choice for pavement and other hard surfaces. Because they are at least partially made of a mesh-style material, they are typically fast-drying. They come in a variety of stability and cushion options.
- *Low-cut hiking boots or trail running shoes* are great for walking, trail-running, day-hiking, and ultralight backpacking because they have the most flexible soles, are the lightest weight, but are only minimally supportive.
- *Mid-cut day-hiking/backpacking boots* require only a small amount of time to break them in, are suitable for day-hiking, lightweight backpacking, and are moderately supportive.
- *High-cut backpacking/mountaineering boots* are great for heavy loads, multi-day backpacking trips, and are the

most supportive. However, they are the heaviest option and have much stiffer soles.

FOOTWEAR MATERIALS:

- *Full-grain leather* needs the most break-in time and has the most water-resistance but is relatively heavy and the least breathable.
- *Nubuck leather* is quite common and has most of the same qualities as full-grain leather but with slightly more flexibility and a rough texture.
- *Split-grain leather* typically is lighter weight but has less resistance to abrasion and water.
- *Synthetic materials* are usually much lighter, need little to no break-in time, and cost significantly less; however, they are much less durable.
- *Vegan* footwear is made from synthetic materials without any animal ingredients or animal byproducts.
- Many boots are labeled *"waterproof and breathable"* because they have a waterproof membrane lining, such as the brand Gore-Tex® or eVent®.

PARTS OF THE SHOE: THE MIDSOLE

The *midsole* provides the cushioning that prevents your feet from feeling every rock and root and creates rigidity in the shoe or boot. A stiffer boot will give you more stability and acts as a shock absorber. A more flexible midsole will be less stable and provide less cushion on rough terrain. The midsole is frequently made of a polyurethane material or ethylene vinyl acetate (EVA).

PARTS OF THE SHOE: OUTSOLES

The *outsole* of a hiking boot is made of rubber and sometimes mixed with other materials for durability. The pattern on the outsole is called a lug pattern. The deeper and thicker the lugs are, the more traction the boots will have. Usually, only backpacking or mountaineering boots will have very thick, deep lugs. If the lug pattern is spaced very close together, they will get packed with dirt much quicker.

SOCKS & OTHER SHOE-RELATED ACCESSORIES

SOCKS

Next to your walking shoes or boots, socks are the next most essential piece of "gear" you will need. Good quality hiking socks are typically made from synthetic materials or wool. My personal preference is Merino wool, and my all-time favorite brand is *Darn Tough Socks*. How can you not love a company that has a lifetime guarantee on their socks? I have had a couple of pairs already for almost 20 years, and they're still going strong!

When walking anywhere, on a trail or pavement, it is important to have socks that fit correctly and wick moisture away from the feet. The most important thing is to avoid cotton. Cotton will absorb water, cause friction, and has no insulating value. If it is cold, this could lead to hypothermia, even in warm temperatures. Oh yeah... and they will take forever to dry and will eventually chafe even the toughest skin on the feet.

Choose wicking materials, such as Merino wool or synthetics like nylon blends. Wool sounds like an unpleasant choice for warmer months, but the benefits far outweigh any negative characteristics in reality. I find they are no hotter than any other sock, and modern knitting technology has made Merino wool socks quite soft and comfortable. It is all I wear year-round.

Properly fitting socks are snug, without being too restrictive, but even more importantly, not too big. You do not want any material bunching up inside your shoe or boot, particularly around the heel. Bunchy socks are one of the most common and avoidable blister-forming blunders. Even socks that once fit well can become loose with wear and cause new problems.

SOCK LINERS
Sock liners are very thin socks, about the thickness of a dress sock or a pair of tights. They are made of wool or synthetic wicking materials that feel a bit "slippery." I am a huge fan of liners that are "toe socks," meaning they have a space for every individual toe. They work wonders!

Sock liners are an excellent "tool" for the footcare toolbox, and if you have any type of blister issues, I highly recommend giving them a try. The beauty of sock liners is that they are very light and dry quickly. If you are on a multi-day hiking trip, except for the most humid areas, if you rinse them out at night, they will usually be dry by morning.

SHOE INSERTS
Shoe inserts, or insoles, are genuinely useful and may help add more support, comfort or adjust the fit of your footwear. These things are not made all the same, just like feet.

Plantar fasciitis is a common and excruciating problem for many avid walkers. The simple answer is that a lot of the time, people merely need more arch support. There are many different brands of inserts on the market today. I am a great fan of *Soles* brand insoles and have a pair in every pair of shoes I wear. You might need more or less support for your particular feet. I am sorry to be the broken record, but the answer is persistence with trying new things and experimentation! You will find the perfect combination eventually.

HEEL CUPS
Sometimes people with "wide" feet who buy "wide" shoes and boots have an issue with the heel area being too big. Some people with wide feet have narrow heels, go figure. I got the

necessary width in the ball and toe-box areas, but the heel region was sometimes too big and caused my foot to slide around, therefore causing heel issues. This was an ongoing problem when I had to buy men's boots because "back in the day," it was difficult to find larger, especially wider, women's sizes. Thankfully, now it is easy to find all shapes and sizes of women's footwear!

Fortunately, there is a brilliant fix for heel slippage, too. Heel cups are little silicone cups in the shape of a heel that you can put in your shoes or boots to help them fit a narrower heel. I find these to work well when thicker socks, or socks and a sock liner, just don't do the trick by themselves.

FEET ISSUES COULD BE RESISTANCE TO LIFE
The health of our feet is often a sign of our emotional ability to move forward. Our feet are representative of our ability to move toward the future. To keep moving forward, despite not always seeing the path clearly, we must learn to embrace the uncertainty of the now. When we feel afraid to take leaps of faith, we stumble around, sometimes literally, off our course of self-evolution.

If you have a problem with your toes or feet or often stumble or bang your toes into things, there could be a message for you hidden in the woes of the toes. If there is something you think about but are afraid to do, or you recognize a repeated cycle of inaction in your past, know that feet issues typically clear up immediately when we begin to follow our hearts instead of our minds. And of course, walking always helps anything, physically, mentally, and spiritually. So, it is important to keep ourselves motivated and enthusiastically moving toward our dreams. Your feet will happily follow your lead.

Chapter 9
WILD CREATURES AND BITEY THINGS

Why walk?
I Awaken! And look it square in the eyes!
Awareness is
being a witness to life,
feeling fully at ease,
It is as if we are returning to peace, over and over again.
Synchronizing the breath with each step,
putting the stick down on the Earth in a rhythmic fashion,
footfalls in a universal march...
It is Sacred Movement in its simplest form.
Time is not of the essence.

WALKING IN BEAR COUNTRY

Bears are truly remarkable creatures. Seeing one can be a magical experience when viewed from an appropriate distance and with thoughtful consideration. When hiking in bear country, some precautions need to be taken so you can enjoy all the wildness of nature without fear. Bears are typically scared of humans and will scurry off at the slightest hint of your presence. However, there are occasions when they can be startled, curious, or defensive and act in less predictable ways.

The type of bears you may encounter will largely depend on your location. The American black bear has the most extensive range of all the bears and is the most commonly seen. In the United States, they inhabit areas as far north as Canada and in the south as far as Mexico. They are quite common in the east and the west from the Rockies to Alaska.

Part of planning and preparing is finding out what regulations concerning bears are in place at your destination before heading out into the backcountry. Some locations require you to carry a bear canister while backpacking and others only ask that you hang your food or possibly your entire backpack.

Like grizzlies, black bears can range in color from light brown to black, although they tend to be almost always black in the eastern United States. Black bears have ears that stand more erect, have an overall more pointed face, and are missing the indicative shoulder hump that grizzly, brown bears, and polar bears have. Grizzly bears are most commonly found in Alaska, western Canada, Wyoming, Montana, Idaho, and Washington.

You can avoid startling bears by frequently making noise, singing, clapping your hands, or banging your hiking poles together while you walk. Bears are most active at dawn and dusk. The incentive for bears to become aggressive is typically situations where you find yourself between a mama bear and her cubs or a source of food.

WHAT DO I DO WHEN I SEE A BEAR?
Never run away because this can trigger an animal's instinct to give chase. Slowly back away and give all bears a wide berth. While most of the time they will immediately scamper away, you will occasionally encounter a more curious black bear.

In a black bear encounter, avoid direct eye contact, make yourself look as large as possible, yell loudly, bang your hiking poles together, or whatever is handy to make a lot of noise. The number of black bear-related deaths (less than 70 since 1900 in the U.S.) is minute compared to the millions of people walking around in bear territory every year. Hopefully, a little information can reassure and help you embrace wildlife encounters as the rewarding gift that it is.

In Grizzly country, it is recommended that you carry bear spray, which is effective at 15- 30,' depending on the brand, and will discharge a continuous stream of concentrated pepper spray. It is crucial to know when and how to use it properly, being especially careful to remain upwind of the stream. It is not recommended to carry a gun in the backcountry. Besides being ridiculously heavy, it has been repeatedly proven that utilizing bear spray is much more effective than attempting to deter a grizzly bear attack with bullets.

In a Grizzly bear encounter, do not run, avoid eye contact, and back up slowly as long as the bear is not approaching you. It is impossible to outrun a bear, so stand your ground, and wave your arms around. If a grizzly bear begins to charge, use your pepper spray when you are within range. If you are attacked, curl up in a ball, or lie flat on the ground with your legs spread apart so the bear cannot roll you over. Remain as calm as possible and try not to panic. Play dead for as long as the bear is in the vicinity.

> *"Walks. The body advances, while the mind*
> *flutters around it like a bird."*
> —Jules Renard

OTHER STINGERS, RASHES, AND BITEY THINGS

BUGS and BITEY THINGS
(More treatment information can be found in the First Aid section)
Other than the irritation of itchy insect bites, the biggest concern is the numerous diseases transmitted by mosquito bites, such as malaria, West Nile virus, encephalitis, dengue fever, and a host of others. Ticks can transmit Lyme disease, Rocky Mountain Spotted Fever, Babesiosis, and several other serious diseases. The best way to avoid these illnesses is to protect yourself with proper clothing and repellant methods.

AVOIDING THE BITEY THINGS
Wearing light-colored, tightly woven clothing with long sleeves and long pants tucked into your socks is the best way to avoid being bitten or stung by anything. Please know, the fashion statement you are making is a minimal cost to preventing Lyme disease!

Tick and mosquito-borne disease prevention include using insect repellent such as 35% DEET or picaridin, which have been proven safe for occasional use on skin, as well as treating clothing with Permethrin. There are plenty of all-natural insect repellents that use essential oils that have mixed results for people. Natural treatments have worked moderately well for me, but I understand I must reapply them much more frequently than chemical options.

Other tactics for preventing mosquito bites is to physically avoid areas with standing, stagnant water, which is where mosquitos breed, and taking extra precautions at dawn and dusk when they are the most active. Also, avoid walking through thick vegetation and tall grass, as these are common hiding places for ticks. Be sure to do a thorough "tick search" after a walk or a hike. Tick-borne diseases require the tick to stay attached for 24 hours or more; However, mosquito-borne diseases can be transmitted instantly.

TREATING STINGS AND BITES

There are several effective ways to stop the stinging and itching from bug bites and bee stings. Washing the area with soap and water is an excellent place to start. Common remedies include applying baking soda, Aloe Vera (a natural antiseptic), lime or lemon juice (contains anti-inflammatory and anesthetic properties), honey, various essential oils, *Calamine* lotion, and other over the counter (OTC) medications. I keep an *AfterBite* pen in my First Aid kit, and it works wonders on stings and bites!

There is a percentage of people that are allergic to bee stings and other insects and develop a variety of symptoms indicating a mild allergic reaction all the way to complete anaphylaxis with major critical system problems. The signs and symptoms can range from itching, hives, and swelling, to a tight, scratchy throat with respiratory distress, nausea, vomiting, and altered mental status.

Wilderness protocol for anaphylaxis recommends:

- Epinephrine: *EpiPen* and *Adrenaclick* are common brand names for this prescription medication in a premeasured auto-injector pen.
- Diphenhydramine: Benadryl is a common brand name for this OTC medication and is usually available in capsule form.

- Prednisone: A prescription steroid medication that usually comes in tablet or pill form.

If you have a history of allergic reactions, it is essential that you always carry the appropriate medication in your First Aid kit. *Safely evacuate any person having a severe allergic reaction or anaphylaxis symptoms, as they can get worse with time.*

POISON IVY & OTHER ITCHY RASHES

Poison ivy is found in every state in the United States (except Alaska and Hawaii) but is most commonly found in eastern states. Poison ivy has three glossy, large-toothed leaves and can be a ground-dwelling plant or a climbing vine. In the fall, the leaves turn red and grow white berries. In the spring, the leaves are shiny, light green with white to greenish flowers.

Poison ivy is commonly found along the edge of trails, rivers, lakes, and other damp areas. Have you ever heard the phrase, "Leaves of three, let it be?" Although there are plenty of non-dermatitis-forming three-leaved plants, until you learn to positively identify poison ivy (hopefully not the hard way!), this is excellent advice.

Although poison oak is occasionally found in eastern states, it mostly grows in the western United States. It also has three leaves that are shaped like oak leaves. It grows as a small shrub or on a long climbing vine and has white or yellow berries. It causes similar effects to other poisonous plant rashes. Poison Sumac is a small shrub or tree and has reddish stems with typically six to twelve leaves.

The allergic reaction is caused by getting the oily sap, called Urushiol, on exposed skin. It can linger on clothing, pets, tools, walking sticks, or other items that have come in contact with the plant. The oil will remain on any surface until it is removed by washing with water and soap or rubbing alcohol. The rash is not contagious and will only surface where the oil has physically come in contact with skin and cannot be spread by scratching.

AVOIDING THE ITCHY THINGS

Avoid poisonous plant rashes by learning how to positively identify the plants in all stages. Wash your clothing, gloves, tools, and hiking poles regularly. Like avoiding insect and tick bites, wear long sleeves and long pants tucked into your socks to avoid coming in direct contact with them. If you do touch it, wash your skin thoroughly with soap and cool water as soon as possible. There are products available now that you can apply to the skin as a barrier to prevent the oil from getting directly on your skin.

Relieve the itch of poisonous plant rashes by soaking in a cool bath, applying colloidal oatmeal, baking soda, OTC calamine lotion, zinc oxide, or OTC corticosteroid medication. Some cases with extreme symptoms, such as high fever, respiratory distress, insomnia, or infection in the eyes, mouth, or cover a large percentage of the body, need immediate medical attention. Prescription oral corticosteroid medication is typically prescribed in these cases.

SNAKEBITES

Although extremely rare, I included a section on snakebites because snakes can trigger mild to extreme fear in many people. Having a little knowledge can sometimes quell the great concerns of the unknown. In a year, only one in 50 million people die from snakebites in the United States. However, it is always a good idea to admire venomous snakes from a safe distance.

There are only two types of venomous snakes found in North America, Coral snakes and pit vipers. Coral snake venom is the only snake venom that is a neurotoxin, which causes interference with the nervous system, paralysis, and muscle spasms. Coral snake bites are extremely rare, perhaps a couple of dozen bites per year in the U.S., and typically occur while being handled.

Pit vipers include rattlesnakes, cottonmouths, and copperheads, and the amount of venom injected is dependent on the size of the snake and its general condition. The antivenin is the same for all members of the pit viper family, so it is not necessary to identify or kill the snake and bring it with you for treatment. The venom is a toxin that causes local tissue damage and swelling. Fatalities are extremely rare. Occasionally, snake bites are "dry bites" where no venom is injected. This may be the case if no symptoms are apparent, such as pain, bleeding, or swelling, within a few hours of the bite.

HOW DO I TREAT A SNAKEBITE?
First of all, do not treat a snakebite like they do in the movies! Do not cut, incise, or suction the wound, as this has been proven to be not only ineffective but possibly harmful. Also, do not apply ice or any type of tourniquet.

The general treatment is to handle the bite as a puncture wound and get the patient to a medical facility so antivenin can be administered as soon as possible. Anticipate swelling by removing any restrictive clothing or jewelry and regularly mark the progression of swelling on the extremity with a pen.

HOW DO I AVOID A SNAKEBITE?
The best protection is to remain aware of your surroundings and watch where you step. Poking the ground near logs and high grass with a walking stick before you take a step will alert any obscured wildlife to your presence. There is clothing that can be worn specifically designed to protect you from snakebites, but it is generally very heavy and bulky. Paying attention to your environment is a much lighter and cheaper option. Being observant will allow you to have total peace of mind and enjoy any wildlife you may encounter.

"The mountains are calling, and I must go."
—John Muir

Chapter 10
BASIC FIRST AID
FOR THE MOST COMMON
BACKCOUNTRY ISSUES

Why walk?
When I have all that I need strapped to my back
such as an apple and a blanket,
I can take my time
and lollygag
and sit next to the stream without a care in the world.
Because I know
That all is well, and all my worries will be waiting for me
Right where I left them.
But for now, I am here
in another world,
And walking can lead me home
When the time is right.

Having a good understanding of First Aid and safety protocols contributes significantly to a fun and stress-free time outdoors. When you have reliable information about what to do in an emergency, it is incredibly empowering and can even be lifesaving. Training for my Wilderness First Responder (WFR) Certification was one of the best decisions I have ever made.

You don't necessarily need a course as extensive as a WFR certification to feel comfortable and informed about potential risks and safety issues. Personal experience is always the best instructor. The following section mentions introductory information about a few of the most common conditions you may encounter while hiking. However, consider taking a basic First Aid course to learn how to use medical supplies and manage everyday wilderness issues.

FIRST AID KIT RECOMMENDATIONS
Although countless items could be in your First Aid kit, only pack things that you know how and when to use. There are many different pre-made emergency kits available for purchase. Make sure the one you choose contains supplies specific to you and your group's needs.

Considerations such as the group's size, the length, and location of your trip, individual medical concerns such as allergies, asthma, diabetes, etc., are the top priorities. It may be most efficient to start with a pre-made kit and customize it for your particular needs.

COMMON FIRST AID KIT CONTENTS
- Pocket Wilderness First Aid Field Guide
- Scissors
- Tweezers
- Safety pins
- Various Sterile Dressings

- Adhesive bandages in sizes small to large
- Sterile Gauze pads, gauze roll, 4 x 4 pads, triangular bandages
- Butterfly wound closure strips
- Moleskin or Molefoam
- Gel blister pads
- Medical/Athletic tape
- Elastic bandage
- SAM Splint
- Gloves
- Disposable thermometer
- CPR mask
- Irrigation Syringe
- Antibiotic Ointment
- Antiseptic (Povidone-iodine solution, ethyl alcohol, hydrogen peroxide)
- Medications:
- NSAIDs (Ibuprofen, aspirin, Naproxen sodium), Acetaminophen, Paracetamol, others
- Antidiarrheal (Imodium A.D.)
- Diphenhydramine- allergy (Benadryl)
- Prescription medication (EpiPen, Rescue Inhaler, etc.)

SUPERFICIAL WOUNDS, BLISTERS, AND BURNS

Blisters are by far the most common issue you or someone in your group is likely to encounter. Although it sounds benign enough, blisters can become serious issues if they become infected, in addition to causing much pain and restricted mobility.

What stage the blister is in when you discover it will determine what treatment to use. If you are vigilant about monitoring your feet for pain and discomfort and employ the "shoe-off-break" technique, you will most likely catch forming blisters in the hotspot stage. Hotspots are red, irritated patches of skin that might actually feel hot, as the name implies.

HOTSPOTS

A hotspot is the easiest to remedy because all you need to do is to stop the friction from causing a full blister from forming. There are several different methods you can use depending on the conditions and length of the hike.

Sometimes the easiest remedy is the best solution. Adding another sock (or a sock liner if you happen to have one with you) can be a simple fix that eliminates any rubbing inside of a shoe. This is another great reason to bring an extra pair of socks. However, if the skin is more than just slightly irritated, you will need to apply some type of cushioning to the hotspot.

One useful type of bandage is a gel blister pad. Currently, there are several reputable brands of these on the market today. Be careful when removing these pads as they are very sticky and can damage the tender skin if they are ripped off too quickly. I have had great personal success with gel pads for blisters and burns, and they stay on for days when you are on a multi-day hike.

Another method of protecting a hotspot is first to apply a minimal amount of skin lubricant, such as antibiotic ointment. If you use too much around the surrounding area, you may cause the adhesive bandage to not stick properly. Cover the whole area with a dressing to protect it from further chafing or apply a smooth tape such as Athletic Tape (my favorite), KT tape, or another type of medical tape.

Typical *Band-Aid* style bandages have their place in a First Aid kit. However, I do not recommend using them on the feet by themselves, as they generally don't stay on and can quickly become an additional irritant floating around the inside of your sock.

FULL-ON BLISTERS

A fully developed blister requires a little more attention to keep it protected from infection and prevent further pain. If you are somewhere that you will need to put your boots back on and keep walking, you will need to unroof the blister and dress it appropriately. Just as you would handle superficial wounds, abrasions, and minor burns, unroofed blisters need to be thoroughly cleaned, disinfected, and dressed. Until they are open, a blister is sterile.

Begin by sterilizing a pin or a needle with a flame and/or antiseptic and make a tiny hole at the base, being careful to leave the skin intact. If the blister was already open when you discovered it, remove any loose, dead skin before applying antiseptic and bandages. After draining any remaining liquid, clean and irrigate the whole area with soap and potable water and cleanse it with an antiseptic.

Use a small amount of antibiotic ointment only on the wound itself. Again, if you use too much around the surrounding area, you may cause the adhesive bandage to not stick properly. Monitor the site for signs of infection, clean, and redress the wound daily.

You can remove the source of friction by using some padded dressing instead, such as *Moleskin, Molefoam, or a gel cushion pad.* Cut out a donut-shaped piece of Moleskin the size of the actual blister or use a non-medicated donut-shaped corn/callous pad, to protect it. Then, apply a small sterile bandage and cover the whole area with medical tape. Or you can use one of the gel blister/burn adhesive pads mentioned above. They can stay on up to two or three days, again being very careful when you go to remove them.

If you repeatedly get blisters in the same area, especially on both feet, it could be an "equipment failure," such as the shoe or boot itself, your socks, or even an insert you are using. Never ignore any pain, discomfort, numbness, or tingling in your feet. These are all signs that your feet need attention. **(See the FEET chapter for detailed information.)**

WOUNDS AND BURNS

Just as you would treat open blisters, clean and irrigate any wound with soap and potable water, remove any debris or foreign objects, and apply antibiotic ointment. Cover the wound or burn with a sterile dressing and use whatever adhesive tape you prefer to keep the bandage in place.

Large wounds and burns are higher risk problems. Fever, disproportionate pain, uncontrolled bleeding or fluid loss, and progressing signs of infection are potentially life-threatening issues and should be treated as such. For these situations, it is essential to get the patient advanced medical care as quickly as possible.

PAIN MANAGEMENT

Pain has the distinct purpose of alerting us that there is something wrong in the body. It is both a symptom of a problem and an issue to be treated. Once you identify and remedy the source of the problem, the goal becomes managing the pain to a tolerable level.

Pain medication falls into two categories; *anesthetics*, which temporarily numb and deactivate nerve cells, and *analgesics*, which systemically reduce pain perception by the brain and the rest of the central nervous system. Both are very useful and sometimes even used together. It is a good idea to have a variety of over the counter (OTC) pain medications, as well as any medication you have been prescribed, in your First Aid Kit. Anesthetics, such as lidocaine or benzocaine, are usually topical anesthetics that numb the pain at the wound location.

Analgesics are classified into three groups: Non-Steroidal Anti-inflammatory Drugs (NSAIDs), opioids, and other nonopioid analgesics. NSAIDs most commonly include Ibuprofen, Aspirin, and Naproxen sodium. Although these medications work in slightly different ways, they are all beneficial for reducing pain, fever, and inflammation. Ibuprofen is one of the most common OTC anti-inflammatory medications and can be quite effective for adults at therapeutic doses of 600-800mg (maximum) every 8 hours.

The benefit of non-steroidal drugs like Ibuprofen is that they are readily available without a prescription. Another advantage is keeping the patient alert and functional, which can be extremely important in a backcountry setting. The most concerning side effects of NSAIDs are bleeding and stomach irritation.

Acetaminophen, also called Paracetamol, is a nonopioid analgesic pain medication that does not have these side effects and is also an excellent pain reliever and fever reducer. However, acetaminophen will not reduce inflammation and swelling like NSAIDs.

Opioids, such as Hydrocodone, Morphine, or Oxycodone, work by reducing the brain's ability to receive pain impulses from the location of the wound. Other opioid side effects, in addition to reduced brain function, are drowsiness, increased reaction time, depressed respiratory function, constipation, and a suppressed response to cold. These can cause significant additional problems in a hazardous backcountry situation.

Having acute or chronic pain, for any reason, can make life challenging. Having supplies for an assortment of potential problems will make any emergency easier and less stressful to resolve. Do your research about the medications you keep in your kit and have a good understanding of the indications, contraindications, dosage, side effects, and possible interactions. Check the expiration date regularly on all your First Aid provisions and restock anything that gets used.

SPRAINS, STRAINS, & BREAKS

Sprains affect tendons and ligaments, strains affect muscles, and breaks involve the bones in the body. You can lessen your chance of having these injuries by utilizing a few techniques. Wear sturdy, supportive footwear, and keep your shoes tied comfortably snug. Use hiking poles and be mindful of where you are stepping. Be extra careful when walking on trails with heavy leaf cover, as you may not see rocks or roots beneath them. Develop a regular stretching routine, such as yoga, to keep your joints flexible and limber.

Whether it is a sprain, strain, or break in the backcountry, the main objective is to minimize swelling, reduce pain, and get the patient to medical care with minimal risk. For soft tissue injuries, use snow, ice, or cold water to reduce swelling. Wrap in a bandage or piece of cloth loosely to immobilize the injury. Elevate the injured extremity, rest, and take anti-inflammatory medication to reduce swelling further.

The most common fractures from falls in the backcountry are wrists, arms, ankles, and legs. With any broken bone, gently splint the extremity with a padded splint using a SAM splint, trekking pole, or other makeshift items. Take anti-inflammatories to reduce the swelling, and carefully and loosely bandage the affected area. Transport the patient to medical care as quickly and safely as possible.

HYPOTHERMIA

Hypothermia occurs when there is a drop in core temperature by several degrees. Hypothermia can occur at surprisingly high temperatures, even 60°F, in windy, wet conditions. The severity is assessed from mild to extreme stages and has a progression of dangerous to life-threatening symptoms.

Uncontrolled shivering, slurred speech, cold skin, and slightly impaired judgment are some of the first signs of mild hypothermia. The remedy is to quickly move the person into a warm, dry environment and remove any wet clothing. The first treatment is to keep the person from getting colder by using blankets, sleeping bags, or extra clothing. Hot liquids and food will help elevate the core temperature.

In more advanced stages, the victim is lethargic, disoriented, breathing shallowly, and will have an altered mental state. Shivering will cease, and the body's primary systems will be functioning at a profoundly reduced level. It is imperative to evacuate the person and seek professional medical help immediately.

FROSTNIP/FROSTBITE

Skin that begins to tingle and looks very pale or waxy may have the beginning stages of frostnip. If it feels hard or is completely numb or frozen, it may suggest frostbite. Toes, fingers, and noses are particularly at risk in subfreezing conditions.

Having the proper cold-weather clothing and gear is key to preventing frostbite. If you suspect someone has frostbite, get them into a warm sleeping bag, use skin to skin contact with another person, or immerse the patient in a warm bath, being careful not to burn the skin due to numbness. Transport the patient to medical care as quickly and safely as possible.

GEAR REPAIR KIT

What do you do when your shoulder strap breaks when you are miles from the trailhead? Well, you channel the genius inner-MacGyver, and hopefully, you have a basic gear repair kit in your pack!

Having an additional section of your emergency kit containing a few necessary items for small gear repairs can save the day!

Having a critical strap or zipper break while you are in the middle of nowhere can be easily remedied with a few simple provisions.

- Duct tape (or Gorilla tape, etc.)
- Cable ties (zip-tie)
- Velcro ties
- Extra zippers, etc.
- Resealable bags
- Large Garbage bags
- 50' paracord or other cordage
- Safety pins
- Travel-size Sewing kit

Conclusion
ARE YOU READY FOR THE *REAL* MAGIC?

Why walk?
Walking is a portal
in which we enter with intention
to systematically let go of all that overly complicates life.
Hoarding emotions that we no longer need....
Wreaking all hell in our bodies,
not even realizing we are the ones choosing.
Walking as a Sacred Path is a choice.
An Awareness.
A purpose.
It is looking for the real magic around every corner &
Entering life's divine portal with playful curiosity.
To immerse oneself wholly, in the now,
letting go of all prospects and expectations.
Walking rhythmically, wherever we are,
losing our minds and finding our peace.

ARE YOU READY FOR THE *REAL* MAGIC?

We have all heard over and over that the magic happens outside of our comfort zone, right? Well, it's the truth, but have no fear! Be open to new opportunities, take sensible risks, be willing, and expand yourself. Say *YES!* to life. Evolve. Participate in everything with as much enthusiasm as you can muster. Most importantly, embrace change with a light heart and a keen sense of humor.

> *"In every walk with nature, one receives*
> *far more than he seeks."*
> —John Muir

Walking is a whole-health means to inner and outer well-being, as well as an exciting way to explore our natural, wild places. As your self-confidence grows, you gain the experience, wisdom, and skills for even greater self-discovery. Be curious like a child, channel the free-spirited adventurer within, and forever dream of exploring uncharted territory.

No smartphone app can replace feeling self-reliant in the beauty and magic of nature. Whether you are with a group of friends on a day-hike, a thrilling solo adventure, or just exploring your neighborhood on foot, being prepared and self-disciplined is self-empowering and well worth the effort. I do not doubt for a minute that a daily walk illuminates the path to lasting peace and happiness. Prepare for a remarkable personal transformation. Since you have made it this far and are here right now reading this, there is no going back. You are already on a *Sacred Path*. A magnificent journey awaits you! Godspeed.

Acknowledgements

For most of my life, everyone close to me has been a devoted walker. I am so thankful to my family for initiating me into a lifestyle of walking. I honestly believe it has saved my life and certainly brought much joy, health, and happiness. I would like to acknowledge just a few of the many people that have helped and inspired me along the way...

I am so Grateful to my DAD. He has inspired me in so many ways, and walking is only one of them. He also taught me how important honesty and personal integrity is personally and in business.

My dad was in a horrible car accident years ago. He was hit in the back of the head with a 50lb bag of birdseed and proceeded to have many agonizing years of back pain without much relief. His MRI was not optimistic, and the doctors repeatedly told him he needed surgery. Even though he was a total mess, he refused to go under the knife.

And then he discovered walking. In the beginning, he couldn't walk very far without having numbness, tingling, and pain so severe he would have to sit down, no matter where he was, or he would fall down. It was so sad to watch somebody who had been so active have so much pain and suffering.

Until he didn't.

His daily walks gave him his life back, and he no longer has back pain. He and my stepmother still walk 6 or 7 miles a day, or more, to this day. (He is in his mid-70s at the time of this writing and looks at least 20 years younger!) They make walking their number one priority every day.

The funny thing is that when I was a child, they would literally have to drag me out the door to go for a walk. Before they moved to the beach, they loved walking all over their midtown neighborhood in Atlanta, Georgia, where I grew up. Me? Not so much. I never wanted to go, and whether it was from rebelliousness or flat-out laziness, I don't remember. I suppose I just hadn't found my stride yet. That would come much later.

Thank you, dad and Christy, for all your love, support, inspiration, and encouragement throughout my life. I love you both dearly!

I am so Grateful to my MOM.
My mother is the world's best listener and supporter, and I don't have any earthly idea where I would be today without her. I call her my rock as she is steadfast as my biggest fan. I am so grateful for her unconditional love.

She, too, is a walker and a runner for many years. When I was little, she would run around the basement for only three minutes in the beginning. She slowly added more time and eventually went outside and started running around the neighborhood. It wasn't too long before she ran for miles and miles, and hours and hours. I remember being so annoyed having to wait for her to finish her run, and shower and dress, before taking me wherever I demanded to go. She was passionate and dedicated. She is also in her 70s and looks as young and vibrant as ever. Thank you, mom, for encouraging me to follow my heart with your strength and courage. I love you and I am so proud of you!

I am so Grateful to my late Aunt AHNA. Her spirit name was Ahnaha WhiteFeather, although many knew her only as Ahna or Anne. She was the very first person I ever knew who truly embodied *Walking as a Sacred Path*. She would walk down the beach like an angelic presence, wrapped in her flowy, white clothing, encompassing all that was above, below, and all

About the Author

Collin Chambers is the founder of *WildWood Magic* and is widely recognized for encouraging people to take walks in nature. After losing 100 pounds by adding a daily walk to her life, she now inspires people to find health and happiness through the simple act of walking.

She teaches personal transformation through enchanted journeys in a magical union of *Walking as a Sacred Practice*, Rituals & Ceremony, and Self-Empowering Hiking & Backpacking Programs. Since beginning her career as a hiking guide and coach, owner of an outdoor gear shop, and facilitator of workshops and events, she has helped endless people discover their inner strength and self-confidence.

Her own journey has taken her from hiking 2,180 miles on the Appalachian Trail to mystical sojourns throughout Peru, Nepal, Thailand, Europe, and India. She is a certified Wilderness First Responder, Backcountry Survival Instructor, and a "Leave No Trace" Trainer. She teaches these and other skills through experiential group and one-on-one custom-created programs.

www.ingramcontent.com/pod-product-compliance
Lightning Source LLC
Chambersburg PA
CBHW070804240726
48654CB00007B/209